World Food

MOROCCO

Catherine Hanger

WORLD FOOD Morocco

1st edition

Published by

Lonely Planet Publications Pty Ltd A.C.N. 005 607 983
192 Burwood Rd, Hawthorn, Victoria 3122, Australia

Lonely Planet Offices

Australia PO Box 617, Hawthorn, Victoria 3122
USA 150 Linden Street, Oakland CA 94607
UK 10a Spring Place, London NW5 3BH
France 1 rue du Dahomey, 75011 Paris

Photography

All of the images in this guide are available
for licensing from Lonely Planet Images.
email: lpi@lonelyplanet.com.au

Published

March 2000

ISBN 1 86450 024 7

Printed by

The Bookmaker International Ltd.
Printed in China.

About the Author
Born and bred in Australia, Catherine Hanger studied literature, languages and a bit of law before heading off to Europe to indulge her wanderlust in the first of many travels. Her first proper job was in Hong Kong as editorial assistant for a travel magazine, and she subsequently worked as a journalist and editor for the *Conde Naste Vogue* titles in Australia. She studied photography in Sydney and later Paris, where she lived and worked as a freelance writer and photographer for some time. She has written a number of books on subjects ranging from food and travel to dreams and children. In her time, she was also a pretty handy waitress. Catherine lives in Sydney and has a two-year-old daughter who is her favourite person and best creation. In her very limited spare time she reads, swims and still manages the occasional late night.

About the Photographer
The author, Catherine Hanger, took many of the photographs in this book. The others were supplied by Lonely Planet Images.

About the Linguist
The language sections were compiled by Moncef Lahlou, Director of the Language Centre, Al Akhawayn Univerisity in Ifrane, Camilia Saad and Mohammed El Saafen.

From the Publisher
This first edition of *World Food Morocco* was edited by Olivier Breton and Martin Hughes of Lonely Planet's Melbourne office. Joanne Adams, Wendy Wright and Martin Hughes designed while Lara Morcombe indexed and Natasha Vellelley mapped. Valerie Tellini, Lonely Planet Images, co-ordinated the supply of photographs, and Brett Pascoe did the pre-press work on same. Dora Chai assisted with production. Karin Vidstrup Monk oversaw the production of the language sections, with assistance from Quentin Frayne and Kerrie Hickin. (Kerrie, sorry for spelling your name wrongly in the other books.) Patrick Marris laid out the language sections, and Patrick Witton provided help with proofing and other essential bits and pieces.

Sally Steward, publisher, developed the series and Martin Hughes, series editor, nurtured each book from the seeds of ideas through to fruition, with inimitable flair.

Acknowledgements
Thanks to Allison Jones, London, for helpful suggestions, and Guy Mirabella for design concepts. Warm thanks to Camilia Saad for her extensive efforts at short notice.

From the author: special thanks are due for the help of the Consulate-General of the Kingdom of Morocco in Sydney, Terry Mullane and his assistant Katrine Bryce; to the Office National Marocain du Tourisme in Rabat and Fès, especially Abdelaziz Mnii (and his family); to Aicha el Hamiani, director of the Royal Cooking School in Rabat; to Dr Mohamed Mezzine and his wife, Leila Benkirane of Fès for their esteemed advice and breadth of knowledge; to Moncef Lahlou of Ifrane. To all the kind and hospitable people of Morocco who made me feel so welcome and shared their knowledge with me, thank-you mille fois. Thanks also to Joan Campbell for lending me her knowledge and her books, Margaret Alcock for same, and fellow travellers to Morocco who told me stories and pointed me in many directions. Thanks to Dr Don Drover, a Moroccan culinary adept who gave much advice; and Prue Rushton for reading and commenting on the manuscript. Thank-you, finally, to my daughter, Eloise and my mother, Joan, who let me go away and supported me through the writing of this book.

Warning & Request

Things change; markets give way to supermarkets, prices go up, good places go bad and not much stays the same. Please tell us if you've discovered changes and help make the next edition even more useful. We value all your feedback, and strive to improve our books accordingly. We have a well-travelled, well-fed team that reads and acknowledges every letter, postcard and email and ensures that every morsel of information finds its way to the appropriate people.

Each correspondent will receive the latest issue of Planet Talk, our quarterly printed newsletter, or Comet, our monthly email newsletter. Subscriptions to both are free. The newsletters might even feature your letter so let us know if you don't want it published.

If you have an interesting anecdote or story to do with your culinary travels, we'd love to hear it. If we publish it in the next edition, we'll send you a free Lonely Planet book of your choice.

Send your correspondence to the nearest Lonely Planet office:
Australia: PO Box 617, Hawthorn, Victoria 3122
UK: 10a Spring Place, London NW5 3BH
USA: 150 Linden St, Oakland CA 94607
France: 1 rue du Dahomey, Paris 75011

Or email us at: talk2us@lonelyplanet.com

Contents

MOROCCO

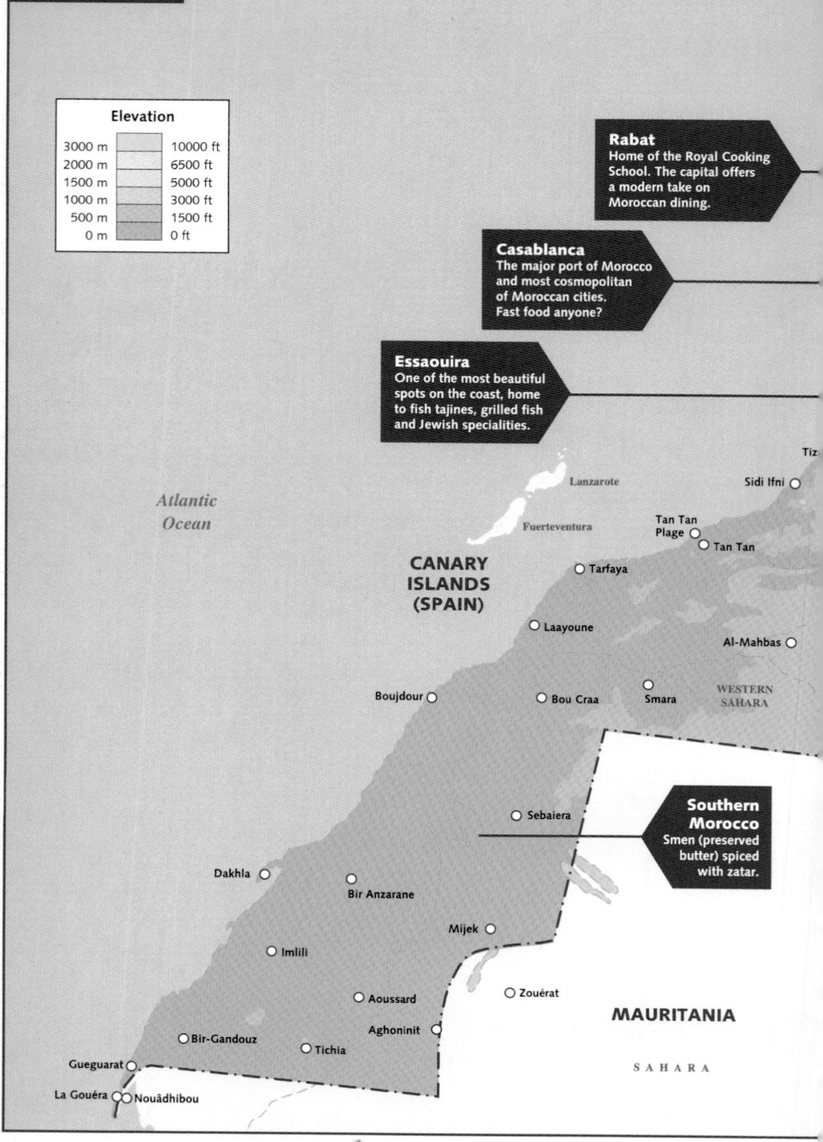
Elevation
3000 m 10000 ft
2000 m 6500 ft
1500 m 5000 ft
1000 m 3000 ft
500 m 1500 ft
0 m 0 ft
Rabat
Home of the Royal Cooking School. The capital offers a modern take on Moroccan dining.
Casablanca
The major port of Morocco and most cosmopolitan of Moroccan cities. Fast food anyone?
Essaouira
One of the most beautiful spots on the coast, home to fish tajines, grilled fish and Jewish specialities.
Atlantic Ocean
Lanzarote
Fuerteventura
CANARY ISLANDS (SPAIN)
Sidi Ifni
Tan Tan Plage
Tan Tan
Tarfaya
Laayoune
Al-Mahbas
Boujdour
Bou Craa
Smara
WESTERN SAHARA
Southern Morocco
Smen (preserved butter) spiced with zatar.
Sebaiera
Dakhla
Bir Anzarane
Mijek
Imlili
Zouérat
Aoussard
MAURITANIA
Aghoninit
Bir-Gandouz
Tichia
Gueguarat
SAHARA
La Gouéra
Nouâdhibou

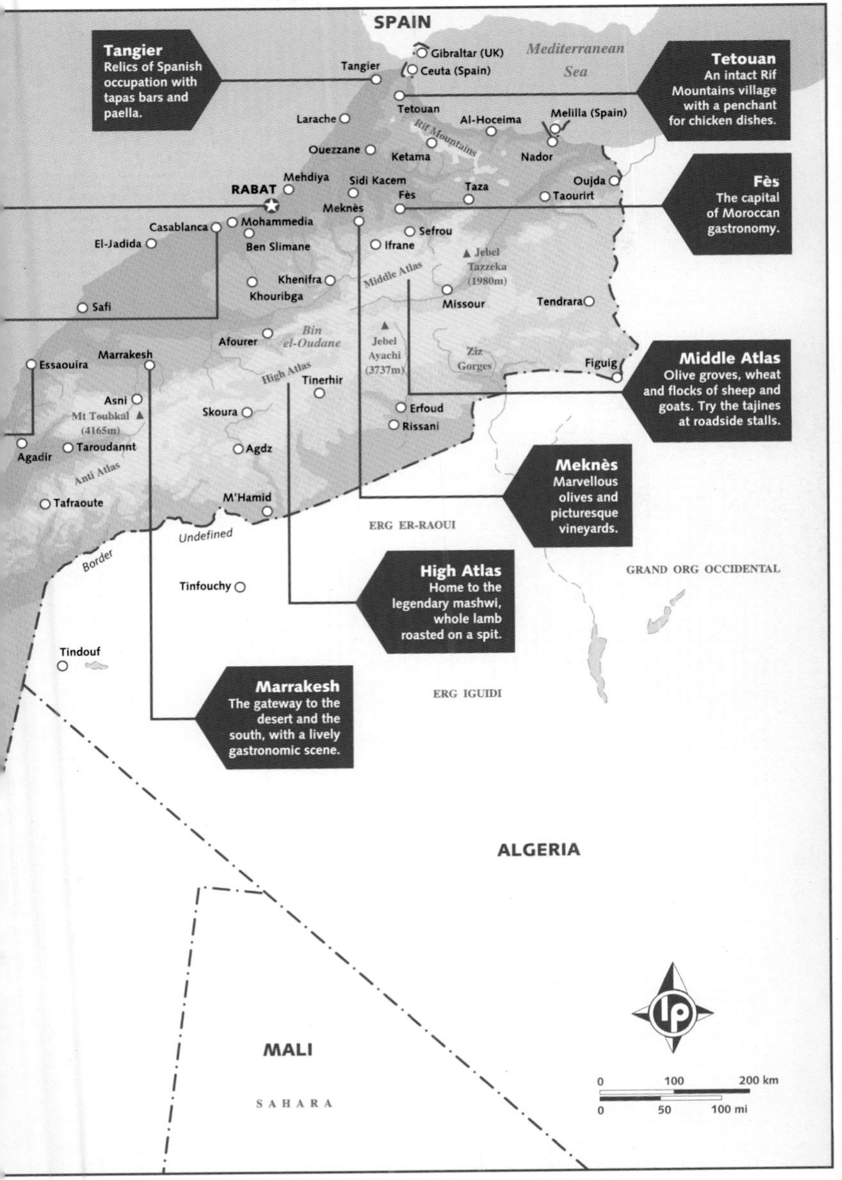

SPAIN
Mediterranean Sea
Tangier
Relics of Spanish occupation with tapas bars and paella.
Tetouan
An intact Rif Mountains village with a penchant for chicken dishes.
Fès
The capital of Moroccan gastronomy.
Middle Atlas
Olive groves, wheat and flocks of sheep and goats. Try the tajines at roadside stalls.
Meknès
Marvellous olives and picturesque vineyards.
High Atlas
Home to the legendary mashwi, whole lamb roasted on a spit.
Marrakesh
The gateway to the desert and the south, with a lively gastronomic scene.
Gibraltar (UK)
Ceuta (Spain)
Tangier
Tetouan
Larache
Al-Hoceima
Melilla (Spain)
Rif Mountains
Ouezzane
Ketama
Nador
Mehdiya
Sidi Kacem
RABAT
Taza
Oujda
Fès
Taourirt
Meknès
Casablanca
Mohammedia
Sefrou
El-Jadida
Ben Slimane
Ifrane
Jebel Tazzeka (1980m)
Khenifra
Middle Atlas
Khouribga
Missour
Tendrara
Safi
Afourer
Bin el-Oudane
Jebel Ayachi (3737m)
Ziz Gorges
Figuig
Essaouira
Marrakesh
High Atlas
Tinerhir
Asni
Mt Toubkal (4165m)
Skoura
Erfoud
Rissani
Agadir
Taroudannt
Agdz
Anti Atlas
Tafraoute
M'Hamid
ERG ER-RAOUI
Undefined Border
Tinfouchy
GRAND ORG OCCIDENTAL
Tindouf
ERG IGUIDI
ALGERIA
MALI
SAHARA
0 100 200 km
0 50 100 mi

Whether it be the simplest dish of couscous and fresh beans, or the glorious and elaborate concoction of a tajine where ingredients are layered with lyrical inspiration, Moroccan cuisine is both distinctive and delicious.

Moroccans are proud of their food. It is invested with all the mythical, religious and ritual significance that a rich culinary tradition attracts. Each major dish has a story or a festival attached, and the sharing of meals is regarded as one of the most important pillars of a society that has, as its central energy, a strong sense of family and tribe.

Moroccan cooks use spices with a heady harmony. Cinnamon, coriander, saffron, mint, cumin, ginger and pepper – the heart of Moroccan food lies in the spice shop. Redolent with tantalising fragrance, colour and warmth, Moroccan dishes orchestrate flavours with a deft touch. Whether in a duet of grilled fish and salad, or the symphony of a **bastila** (pigeon or poultry pie), strong and velvety flavours form an unmistakeable theme.

In Morocco, food is women's work. Women are still very much mistresses of the home and hearth, and cooking remains firmly fixed in the feminine domain. Even the largest and most prestigious of hotels and restaurants will have a battalion of Moroccan ladies in the kitchen. Recipes are not common. Most women know the dishes as a language with which they have been imbued from birth. Each woman will give a dish her own special signature expressed through the subtle differences that arise from region, social standing, personality, or simply whatever catches her fancy in the market that day. Every man in the land knows how to interpret good food.

Anyone who wants to experience the real life of Morocco must visit the **souqs** (markets) that punctuate every village, town and city. Here, all the myriad threads of Moroccan culture converge, from the simplest and most rustic country souq to the grand theatre of the famous market square in Marrakesh. Food is integral – from the earthy vegetables of a rustic farmers trolley to butchers' shops, and from the mouthwatering scent of grilling fish to the fragrance of the stewing tajines.

Eating is a celebration in Morocco, and the sign of a well-ordered life and mind. To Moroccans it represents harmony. Food is family and festivity and one of the most important ways of expressing a cultural tradition that is as rich and varied as the banquets held to celebrate every aspect of life.

the culture of moroccan cuisine

It's all in the hands. There is a magic in Moroccan food, and it comes from the women who make it, from secrets passed on like a sign language, by mothers and grandmothers. These secrets can't be told, only felt through fingertips, and observed over time. Traditionally veiled and closeted, it's little wonder that a Moroccan woman's hands and eyes are her most powerful means of self expression.

Cooking is still very much a woman's craft. Men do not learn it, except through formal avenues. Men taste, judge, and even decide what is to be cooked and how, but they are not usually privy to its process. Such is the importance of food in Moroccan culture that a man can tell much about the upbringing or temperament of the woman who has prepared the dish he is eating, without ever having glimpsed her. In Morocco, food is an integral part of communication between the sexes.

Things are changing, of course – women are becoming more independent, some homes now have refrigerators and freezers, people travel further to work, and families are more fragmented. Moroccan food itself may change but it is likely to be a gentle evolution. Moroccan cuisine is like myth – the story seldom changes, though details vary from time to time, place to place and woman to woman. Moroccans prefer it this way.

Few cookbooks can do justice to the complexity of Moroccan food – knowledge comes from a deeper source. Traditionally, when a young bride went to her new husband's house, she brought with her a heritage of lore learned in the kitchen. Older Moroccan women rarely give precise measurements for ingredients – it's those elements of feeling and watching, combined with such intangibles as mood, weather, seasons and what's available that day at the **souq** (market) that form their expertise.

For Moroccans, food is inseparable from family, and thus sacred. Meal times represent the forum in which the family knows itself. For a traditional Muslim, cuisine carries symbolic and religious significance. Certain foods and dishes are eaten only at specific times of the year, and tradition and rules dictate their presentation and order. Moroccan cuisine expresses and underscores the rules of its society.

To carry on the myth analogy, Moroccan food is quite simple, a fusion of whimsy and practicality depending on ingredients and occasion. Basic themes are few: long, slow cooking of stews and braises with sauces created by reduction; grills; salads of cooked vegetables; bread and cakes from local grains; and fruit. Distinguishing characteristics come through the use of spices – not for heat, but for fragrance and complexity – interleaving the dish with infinite drama and detail. This is where creativity comes in, as each cook tells her own tale.

Internationally, it's a different story. Elements of Moroccan food have been lifted and merged with other factors. Like Italian food, it has been adapted into a multiplicity of themes which have carried the delicious flavours of the country across the world. While these new versions bear little resemblance to traditional cooking methods, there is no mistaking Moroccan influence when it appears in a dish in Sydney, New York or London; the marriage of spices is unmistakable.

Zellige work, Fès

History

Veiled in fragrant spices, replete with a rich array of ingredients, Moroccan food is a window on the history of this fertile land. Despite waves of invaders and the influences they left behind, Moroccan culture has adapted to the times, without losing its integrity.

Morocco's first inhabitants were the Berbers, and their culinary methods survive today. Divided into tribes, they ate what they farmed, bartered or took. Berber cooking used vegetables and pulses of the season with the ubiquitous couscous – often made with cracked maize or barley as well as semolina (see Couscous in the Staples & Specialities chapter). Meat and poultry were less frequently used; chickpeas and beans providing protein. **Khli'** (preserved meat) is a Berber speciality and allows precious meat stocks to be used all year round (see Meats in the Staples & Specialities chapter). Many cooking pots and utensils are Berber in origin: the **tajine**, used to make the stew-type dish named after it; and the portable **majmar** cooker which allowed semi-nomadic families to enjoy good food wherever they were. The famous **mashwi** (barbecued lamb) is also Berber (see Meats in the Staples & Specialities chapter). Couscous with barley shoots, still found in the Rif mountains and Souss area, was another favourite dish. Buttermilk from the herds of sheep and goats became a traditional accompaniment to couscous dishes. The Berber tribes dominated the real life of Morocco despite Phoenician contact with coastal settlements and later, benign Roman rule.

Essentially, there were two outside influences on the development of Moroccan cuisine: the Arab influence drawn from its Persian heritage; and the influences flowing back into Morocco from Spain. The Arab invasion, in the name of Islam, took place in the late 7th century. Horsemen from the deserts of the Middle East overran Morocco and the rest of North Africa without serious resistance, and passed over the Mediterranean into Spain. However, the Berbers ascended once again in 740 AD and Morocco, while Muslim, remained independent. Three centuries of unrest and shifting allegiances followed until the Berbers united under the Almoravids, who enforced rule over all of Morocco and Muslim Spain. The Almohads were the next tribe to take over, but were driven out of Spain in the 13th century.

Trade routes followed the ebb and flow of battles, and Morocco became a major spice user. The Muslim Arabs, in their peregrinations, cross-pollinated culinary cultures from east to west, gleaning spices from China, India and Malaysia. For centuries they were the sole custodians of the spice routes, inventing extraordinary tales to protect their sources. Cinnamon sticks, for example, were said to come from the nests of great birds. The story told by Herodotus, the ancient Greek historian, reports that the birds were tempted by greed to take large joints of meat to their nests – the joints were left by cunning cinnamon harvesters – which broke under the weight. The sticks were then collected and sold by traders.

It was through the mobility of the new and energetic Muslim Arab nation that many spices and recipes were transported to Morocco. The Moroccans assiduously adopted the new sweet and sour combinations, the use of fruits with meat (the desert Arabs were already familiar with the partnership of meat and dates). They took on the fondness for nuts, the attraction to honey and delectable sweetmeats, together with the enthusiastic use of the most fragrant spices, seeking to outdo their antecedents with lavish and extraordinary dishes.

The existence of a rich and ambitious Moroccan court – through the rulers of the Almoravid, Almohad, Merenid and Saadian dynasties – was crucial to the development of Moroccan cuisine as it exists today. While the rich and fertile countryside was able to support the production of meat, vegetables, fruit, olives, nuts and dates, it was the sophistication of the courts in the major imperial cities of Fès, Meknès, Marrakesh and Rabat that developed the rich and lavish culinary tradition.

The court tradition included a serious academic side. Many cookery manuals were written in Baghdad during the 10th to 13th centuries, documenting elaborate dinners and explaining recipes. In tandem with this literary interest in food was a scientific fascination in the newly discovered discipline of dietary medicine, which helped to enhance the reputation of herbs and certain culinary combinations. Elegant poems were written to

RECIPES FOR SUCCESSORS

A gastronomic festival in Fès in 1997 heralded the publication of a book called the *Fudalat al-Khiwan*, written in Arabic in the 13th century by Ibn Razin Tujubian, an Andalucian nobleman. SOme 800 years later, two Moroccan academics, Dr Mohamed Mezzine and his wife, Leila Benkirane, translated this work into French for the first time. In doing so, they refocused attention to Morocco's culinary history. Many of the 414 recipes in the book, however, were still in common usage.

The *Fudalat* is also important because it is the sibling of another crucial Arab culinary text, *A Baghdad Cookery Book*, translated by an Englishman, Professor AJ Arberry, in 1939. The *Fudalat* deals with the Andalucian (Spanish) heritage while the *Baghdad Cookery Book* deals with the Persian heritage of Moroccan cuisine.

various foods and the banquet was connected with the finer instincts of life and love as well as the sheer delight in sensual gratification.

Another major influence on Moroccan food came with the refinements developed in Spain by the Arab controllers, the Moors. Moorish culinary habits were drawn from the Arab-Berber fusion in Morocco, and became strongly entrenched in Spain during Moorish rule. These culinary habits were returned to Morocco when the Moors were finally driven out of Spain.

Boabdil, the last Moorish king, fled to Fès in 1492. He was followed by a large Jewish-Moorish population, who introduced skills in pickling and preserving fruit and vegetables, skills still used today. The Moors were also masters at creating magnificent gardens including those of fragrant citrus and other fruit-bearing trees. Their use of spices had reached great heights of sophistication, and they were highly knowledgable in the use of dietary medicine.

Essentially, the Moors brought a higher consciousness in the culinary arts, as well as specific dishes such as **paella** (a saffron-flavoured rice dish) and some **tapas** (appetisers) which you can still find today in the coastal regions of Morocco's north. The increased production and use of olive oil is another good example of Spanish influence on Moroccan culinary culture.

Later still, the Ottoman Turks introduced grills and barbecues to Morocco's culinary repertoire. The French colonised Morocco in 1912 and strong traces of their 44-year stay are still present, in infrastructure and the use of French terminology. They left behind pastries and desserts, ice creams and confectionery, wine, and the combining of grills with raw salads. More importantly, they introduced certain agricultural practices, which improved land yield.

Agriculture in Todra Gorge, Central Morocco

How Moroccans Eat

Three meals a day is the norm for most Moroccans, with the main meal occurring around midday. Dinner is usually a more casual affair unless it coincides with a special event, or a visitor is present.

Moroccans eat a variety of foods for breakfast, including many western European staples. Toasted bread and cereal is common, especially in hotel restaurants, which may also serve English tea (or 'liptons', as non-mint tea is often called).

A more traditional Moroccan breakfast includes **baghrir** (a semolina pancake made with yeast and cooked on one side only with a distinctive honeycomb appearance), **malwi** or **rghayif** (variations of dough folded and interleaved with butter or oil, which creates a flaky texture) served with **khli'** (preserved meat).

Moroccan women begin preparing the midday meal as soon as breakfast is over. Tajines, salads and couscous can take hours to cook, and there is often shopping to be done beforehand. The midday meal is large and multi-faceted. The family is expected to meet, eat a lot, and relax, before returning to work later in the day, a tradition common to all Mediterranean countries. Subsequently, many businesses shut down for the midday period. Most family members – distance from work permitting – return home for lunch. Most unmarried Moroccans live *en famille* so eating with the family group is a strong patterned custom.

TRAIN SWAPPING

We knew about the Moroccan custom of sharing food with fellow travellers, but in our scramble to catch the train we neglected to stock up on provisions. If our luck held out, we thought, no one would offer us anything and we wouldn't be caught with nothing to share.

To our dismay, a family sat opposite and began offering us fruit and bread. Then, two young boys raced through our car selling bars of chocolate. Realising that a solution to our problem was at hand, Mark chased after the boys but couldn't find them. A man standing at the end of the car explained to him that the boys were hiding in the rest room to avoid the ticket taker. He offered to broker a deal for the chocolate. I was politely declining the umpteenth offer of an orange when Mark returned with his bounty. We had sticky orange juice fingers for the rest of our long trip to Fès but the chocolate-smeared smiles of the children more than made up for it.

Cheryl Kohler

Street stall, Place Djemaa el-Fna, Marrakesh

Due to the size of the midday meal, dinner is usually a simpler affair, although if you are the guest of a Moroccan family, prepare yourself for yet another major feast. In families, most partake of whatever is left from lunch, with perhaps a salad, omelette or grilled meat.

Snacks, in the western sense, have no place in traditional Moroccan cuisine although the likes of lollies and crisps are turning up in corner shops. Dried fruit and nuts sometimes fill the gap but the little bowls of nuts you may see are mainly for visitors. These may be served with biscuits and cakes at morning or afternoon tea, accompanied, as always, by mint tea. The sequence and balance of Moroccan meals are so well tuned that snacks are generally unnecessary and, certainly in poorer rural communities, the opportunity for snacking in terms of time or resources is minimal.

FOODS FOR PREGNANCY

While pregnant women will not be denied their cravings, they are usually discouraged from taking certain foods. If she eats snails it is feared that the baby may end up with similar characteristics; and if she eats strawberries, the baby may be born with ugly birthmarks. To this end, such foods are avoided by the entire household or hidden, since a pregnant woman must not be refused her desires.

The Arab Tradition of Hospitality

The Moroccan tradition of hospitality is legendary and deeply rooted in the community. Sacred law states that visitors must be shown a suitable welcome, which means that they are offered the best possible food and lodging. This law is enshrined to the extent that an extra serving is always prepared, whether visitors are expected or not.

The serving is symbolic, but some travellers have even reported an extra place being set at the table. The leftover food is never wasted and it's usually included in the next meal. In any event, the object is that everyone will have more than enough to eat. If there aren't any scraps, it means the cook hasn't prepared enough.

Incidentally, hospitality does not end at the table. When visiting a Moroccan home, be careful not to comment too favourably on any decorative elements, clothes or indeed anything portable – you may have to carry it with you. Refusal of such a gift is considered very uncouth.

This tradition is thought to have its origins in the Arab fear of the evil eye – the envied object is given away to deter jealousy. Moroccans would not necessarily rationalise giving in this way. They give because generosity is a highly regarded part of their culture. This is also why you'll rarely hear a host boasting about the food or quality of his wife's cooking. If anything, judgement is reserved, which can sometimes make the family appear critical.

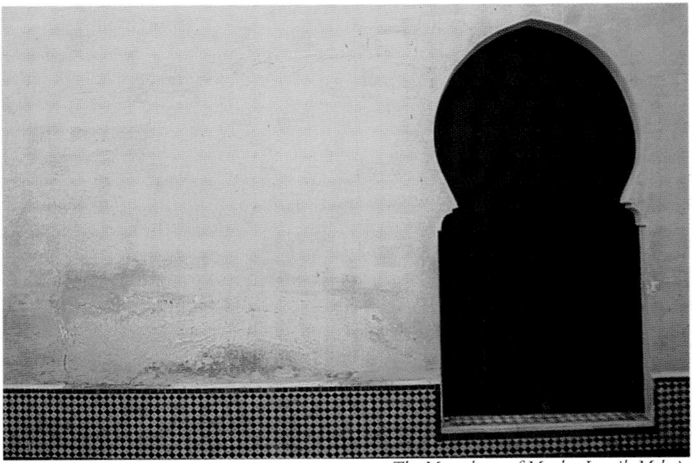

The Mausoleum of Moulay Ismail, Meknès

You'll experience this generosity first hand in any Moroccan home. Don't expect to get away without being offered copious quantities of mint tea – three glasses at one sitting is acceptable – and a meal. If you had no intention of sharing a meal, it is polite to refuse food at first, and then to give in with some reluctance and much grace. You'll have to eat something as the host is obliged to offer you food and drink as soon as you enter the home. Outright refusal would be considered extremely rude.

Chances are that you'll be invited for a meal. In this case, you should bring a gift – biscuits or confectionery for example. On receipt, your host will probably offer you some of your own gift.

Whatever meal you're served in a Moroccan home, it will be the best the host can afford. Your host will insist you eat the best portions by serving them to you. Once again, don't refuse anything. This may be a problem if you're offered something that you detest but an appreciative taste, at least, is required. If you fail to taste something that others at the table have, they'll feel very uncomfortable. If you are vegetarian, you should state your preferences beforehand.

Remember that to properly honour a guest, the host must over cater. For a guest to leave the table even slightly dissatisfied is shameful, so the more dishes the better. At the end of the meal, a significant portion of food must remain.

Hospitality also extends to conversation. It is incumbent on the host to be cheerful, avoid serious or controversial topics, and keep the conversation relatively light. He must not disagree with his guest.

The good guest should be talkative, and prepared to praise the food and admire the manners of host and family.

FOOD FOR FRIENDS

In Morocco, public spaces are usually crowded with men; home for many of them is where they eat and sleep. The home is where women spend much of their time, and a regular highlight for women is visiting friends. Afternoon – after the family has been fed – is the most popular time for visiting. While Moroccan hospitality demands that visitors are fed, women friends don't make the same fuss over one another as they would strangers. That said, delicious **berkoush** (rice pudding made with milk) is a popular accompaniment to spontaneous visits. It's simple, cheap, quickly made and perfect for convivial company.

Margo Daly

Man wearing winter djebella

Etiquette

Guests are usually entertained in the most lavishly decorated room in the house. This room is lined with couches, upholstered in the most sumptuous fabric family finances will allow. Guests are expected to sit on the couches or on large cushions. The tea ceremony takes place on the low tray table. In more modern or less formal settings, the tea, already made, may simply be presented in glasses, having been prepared in the kitchen (see Etiquette under Tea in the Drinks chapter).

In a country where eating with hands is a time-honoured tradition, hand-washing is an extremely important part of etiquette. Everyone is expected to wash their hands before a meal. You'll either be invited to wash your hands in the bathroom (often quite ornate because it's customary to wash hands without closing the door) or offered a large copper basin and jug by a maid or child. Whoever is offering the jug will pour rose or orange flower-scented water over your hands and then offer you a towel.

When the meal is ready to be presented, a large, circular table – complete with embroidered tablecloth – is wedged against one of the corners of the room. This allows diners to sit at two sides of the table, while chairs are brought in to complete the table setting. Guests will usually be presented the elegant couch to sit on, although the chairs and cushions are actually more comfortable. Don't be surprised if the women of the house don't sit with you. It is traditional for women to eat separately and at different times to men. However, they seem to make allowances with female visitors, and we were usually joined by the women of the house.

The cook will present the meal, and leave. The host will pronounce, "**Bismillah**" (in the name of Allah), which should be echoed by everyone, after which you may start eating.

The most important rule at the table is to eat only with your right hand. It may help to surreptitiously sit on your left hand, which can only be used for picking up bread or passing other dishes. Furthermore you should only eat with the first two fingers of your right hand, using your thumb as the pincer (three in total). Using more digits is a sign of gluttony but probably unavoidable without practice. Moroccans are usually prepared for the ineptitudes of foreigners. Keep trying but don't use your left hand.

Cutlery may be laid on the table for your benefit, but it is more polite to try to eat with your fingers. The only exception to this is probably couscous which Moroccans expertly roll into balls, a feat which takes years of practice.

Sometimes plates will be set in front of each person, where you place any gristle, bones or other unwanted remnants. If there is no plate, there may be a plastic table covering or communal bowl. Follow your host's lead, or ask.

Bread will be offered to you, or placed strategically where you can reach it. Never help yourself to bread from the receptacle in which it is placed. It is said that if more than one person apportions the bread at the table, the house will be beset by quarrelling. Use your bread to mop up sauces and juices and to help pick up pieces of food.

Eat from dishes in front of you. Don't reach around or dig about. Salads and secondary dishes will either be placed within reach, or passed to you. Your host or a member of the family may assist you by pulling out the best pieces of chicken or the most delicious portion of meat – take it gratefully. It's better to take many small pieces than one large one. It is considered unseemly to munch your way around a large leg of poultry, for example. Moroccan cooking is ideally suited to eating with hands because of the long cooking time. Meat simply melts into the sauce and falls easily off the bone. Leave the whole leg and pull off a smaller piece of meat.

Even if you get full, it's best to continue nibbling at something. If others notice that you have stopped eating they may feel obliged to follow suit and the dishes will be cleared away.

Save licking your fingers until the end of the meal when it is entirely appropriate. If you wish to wipe them during the meal, do so delicately on a piece of bread, or on a napkin.

When eating in a restaurant, you'll most probably be eating western-style even if the environment and cuisine is resolutely Moroccan. It is extremely unusual for Moroccans to eat at restaurants.

WINSTON CHURCHILL'S GAFFE

Winston Churchill dined with a Glaoui chieftain in the south of Morocco. He knew that he was required to wash his hands but didn't know the precise etiquette. Being an honoured guest, he was offered the jug first. He called for soap and washed his hands thoroughly. When it came to the Glaoui's turn, he merely washed the tips of his fingers, and dried them delicately.

As soon as the meal was cleared away, the water jug came round again. This time, Churchill merely washed the tips of his fingers while the Glaoui rolled up his sleeves and thoroughly rinsed his hands up to his forearms.

Moroccans laugh at Churchill's perceived discomfort when they tell this story. The implication was that Churchill – master of the renowned English manners – had come to visit with dirty hands. Moreover, when he really did have dirty hands at the end of the meal, he didn't think to wash them.

Restaurants generally replicate a plush family dining room. Some restaurants are divided into smaller rooms containing only a few tables, which exaggerates this feel by providing a sense of intimacy. While it's rare for Moroccans to eat at restaurants it's even rarer for them to eat as a couple. If you are *a deux*, you may find yourselves seated uncomfortably on a couch, side by side. Don't complain; it's part of the experience.

Restaurant service usually consists of an army of men dressed in traditional garb complete with smart, red Fès cap; or a flock of pleasant-faced young women who are dressed traditionally in full-length **djellabas** (long hooded robes). Tables are usually covered with white or embroidered napery. Napkins are always provided, as is a full set of cutlery. You won't be expected to eat with your hands.

While a restaurant may be a good introduction to Moroccan food, real Moroccan cuisine is only eaten at home and, unless you manage to score an invite, your culinary experience will remain incomplete.

staples
& specialities

As a crossroad between Europe and the Arab world, Morocco has benefited from the new tastes brought by traders and invaders. New spices and specialities, along with native grains and other staples have all played a part in shaping the nation's diverse cuisine. Within Morocco's pantry you will find everything from the sacred date to a complex warqa.

Couscous

Couscous is synonymous with Moroccan food, and is the defining national dish. It is both the basic ingredient – a semolina found in varying forms all over North Africa and native to the region – and the name of a dish, which is the semolina topped with a rich stew.

Other Arab countries have taken couscous and call it **maghrebiyya** (from the region called the Maghreb, denoting the area of North Africa touching the coast of the Mediterranean) but this has little in common with the magnificent couscous prepared in Morocco. Unlike Algerian couscous – where the elements of the meal are served separately and the broth is often heavily spiced with **merguez** (spicy lamb sausage) and fiery **harissa** (rich chilli paste) – Moroccan couscous is usually served as one composite dish. Harissa is not a traditional accompaniment, and hot couscous dishes made with chilli peppers are rare. Most Moroccan couscous is perfumed, spiced and fragrant, but not hot. The dish can include any number of elements from meat and seasonal vegetables, to dried fruit and nuts. It can be sweetened with sugar and cinnamon (called **seffa**, this dish is especially popular with children and is served with a glass of milk) and yoghurt for a snack or dessert.

Couscous semolina has also travelled; to Sicily where it is known as *cuscusu*; to Senegal where it is *keskes* and more closely resembles the Moroccan version; and even to Brazil where it is made from maize, rice or tapioca and known as *cuscuz*. It's thought to have been introduced through Portuguese slave ships, and is served with anything from shrimps to chicken. Of all the couscous in this part of the world, the Moroccan variety is widely regarded to be the best.

Pasta is the best culinary analogy for couscous and the roots of both staples converge. Like pasta, couscous is made from a type of hard wheat (although in certain regions of Morocco couscous is also made from barley or corn). Couscous is derived from the purified middle of the wheat grain. Sauces are infinitely varied, depending as much on the cook and her imagination as the availability of seasonal produce, regional variety and cost.

Couscous has changed very little over many centuries. It is originally a native Berber dish, and is known to them as **seksoo** or **sikuk**. It's thought that, originally, couscous was simply adorned with preserved butter called **smen** and accompanied with milk (see Smen under Butter & Yoghurt later in this chapter). Gradually chickpeas, vegetables and meat were added. Couscous later became a fabled dish of the imperial courts. It appeared as a golden mound served at banquets, topped with pigeons (themselves perhaps stuffed with couscous, dates and nuts), succulent lamb, copious spices, or other delicacies such as sheep's head garnished with dried fruits, nuts or preserves.

To make couscous in the traditional way requires patience, rhythm and a great deal of time. The most important element in the making of couscous is the finesse of the woman preparing it. Her taste, eye and above all her hands determine the quality of the dish. Expect more variations of couscous than with any other Moroccan dish.

It may be comforting to know that many Moroccan families now also use packaged 'instant' couscous grains. If treated correctly, the results can be very impressive but, as with traditional couscous, the 'handling' of the convenient variety is still important (see the boxed text Preparing Couscous).

A Sauce for Couscous

Ingredients

3	carrots, cut lengthwise	3	turnips cut lengthwise
3	zucchinis, uncut	2	medium sized tomatoes
½	teaspoon saffron	½	teaspoon ginger

2-4 litres of water
250g pumpkin, cut into large pieces
2 medium sized onions, cut into quarters
1kg mutton, beef or chicken, cut into pieces
1 generous bouquet of parsley and coriander, chopped
2 cups of vegetable oil or melted butter
2 capsicums, cut into large pieces and seeded
half a cauliflower, cut into four pieces
1 cup chickpeas, soaked overnight and strained (or 1 can of prepared chickpeas, strained)
cayenne pepper to taste
salt and pepper to taste

In the bottom half of a couscoussier (or large steamer) put the meat, spices, oil, onions, parsley and coriander. Cover with water and bring to a simmer. Stir and cook for about an hour, during which time the first cooking of the couscous grains should take place.

After the first cooking of the couscous grains, add the vegetables to the stew and stir. Add more water if necessary (not to cover, but about half way up the pot).

Cook for 15-20 minutes. When the stew is almost ready, do the second cooking of the couscous grains.

Pile the prepared grains onto a large, shallow platter and cover with the stew. Serve immediately.

Serves 4-6

Preparing Couscous

This recipe assumes the use of widely available packet couscous.

You will need a couscoussier or a large steamer that is well sealed; if the seal is loose or the holes of the steamer are too large, line the vessel with cheesecloth.

1. Wash the couscous in a shallow pan, sieve it and allow the grains to sit and swell for 10 minutes. At this point start to heat the water in the bottom of the couscoussier so that it's boiling when you need it.
2. With cupped, wet hands, lift the couscous, rub it gently between your hands and let it fall. This will break up any lumps. Then rake the couscous with your fingers.
3. Put about a quarter of the washed couscous into the couscoussier. Let it steam without the lid for five minutes. Pour the rest of the couscous on top and again steam without the lid, this time for about 20 minutes.
3. Remove the top part of the couscoussier and turn out the couscous into a large, shallow pan. Sprinkle a cup or so of water and some salt through the couscous. Oil your hands and gently work the couscous as before. Smooth the couscous out and let it sit for 10 minutes. If it feels dry, add more water in small doses and rake it through. At this point you can cover the couscous and keep it to one side if you are running ahead of time with the accompanying stew.
4. Return the couscous to the steamer as before and steam for a further 20 minutes.

Handling the couscous

In the traditional way, each family sends its wheat to be ground at the local miller. Families are very specific about the coarseness they prefer and instruct the miller accordingly. Once ground, the couscous is rubbed by the cook with fine flour and a little water until each grain is separated and coated with a fine film. This is done in a **gas'a** (a wide, shallow wooden or earthenware bowl) in which the final dish is often served. This process allows the grains to swell and cook when steamed without clumping together in a doughy mass.

The couscous is cooked in a **couscoussier** (a special two-tiered pot), with couscous on the top in the steamer and meat and vegetables simmering below. The fragrant steam impregnates the couscous, which swells and softens after about 40 minutes of steaming and 'handling'.

In Morocco the couscous grain has strong religious and emotional significance. Because of its place at the centre of the cuisine, it holds a symbolic connection to sustenance in its broadest sense. It is cheap, filling and nourishing, and can be used as the base for anything from a simple peasant broth to an extravagant feast of stuffed pigeons.

In this sense couscous is connected with one of the major tenets of Islamic law, the giving of alms. Eaten mainly at the midday meal on Friday, the Muslim day of rest, a plate of couscous is then taken to the local mosque to be distributed among the poor. Many mosques insist that the poor be invited into people's homes and cooks are expected to serve the same fare they would serve their own family. It is frowned upon to make an inferior alms couscous.

Possibly because of its strong connection with humility and nurturing, many Moroccans will tell you that couscous is never a central feature at important ceremonies such as marriages. Couscous is served as only one of many dishes at **diffas** (banquets), and usually at the conclusion of a series of rich **tajines** (stews) to ensure **shabaan** (complete satiation) for all the guests present.

Couscous also has a strong historical connection with **pannades**, an ancient Arabic dish based on leftover bread – itself a revered substance – crumbled finely into simple but nourishing casseroles. It has been said that couscous is the finest sort of pannade. The Prophet Mohammed himself is said to have adored couscous, which is another good reason for any devout Moroccan to enjoy it.

Soups

In a culinary culture where stewed foods have reached their zenith, soups take a secondary role. They are often variations of the renowned **hrira** (thick soup), which is eaten traditionally each day at sundown during the fasting month of Ramadan. Many Moroccans eat hrira throughout the year, but others say that having eaten it every day for an entire month, they are glad not to taste it until Ramadan rolls around again.

Ramadan is the ninth month of the Muslim year (its position in the year changes according to a lunar calendar) and Muslims are forbidden to take food or drink (including water) between sunrise and sunset (see the Celebrating with Food chapter). At sunset, the traditional hrira is served – in homes, restaurants or roadside stops. Dates, honey cakes and, later, coffee or milk usually accompany the soup.

Hrira may also be served by the new wife to her husband's family the day after marriage. This indicates to everyone that the marriage night was a success and that she is no longer a virgin.

Hrira has as many subtleties as there are cooks in Morocco but it usually consists of a broth replete with lamb cubes, chicken giblets, lentils, chickpeas, tomatoes, onions, garlic, fresh herbs and spices (coriander, cinnamon, parsley, smen, sometimes saffron and ginger), rice or **shariyya** (very fine noodles that are often used as a substitute for couscous). The soup is simmered for an hour or two (the lentils and chickpeas determine the time of cooking) and then thickened with yeast or flour before serving. Eggs are sometimes added. Before eating, lemon is squeezed on the soup to taste.

Other popular soups include chickpea, lentil, broad bean and pumpkin, although pumpkins are generally reserved for use in couscous. Nourishing vegetable soups are found in various forms everywhere (usually using a shoulder of lamb or another, similar, cut of meat, for stock).

Soup sometimes plays a medicinal role in Moroccan culture. For example, **nfissat** (a thin but nourishing mutton soup) is served to women who have just given birth while a broth based on toasted aniseed is said to relieve a sore back or cold.

Bread

While waiting to be served mint tea at the spectacular Cafe Maure overlooking the estuary of the river in Rabat, we noticed a well-dressed young man, in western-style clothes, stride purposefully down a narrow street. He came to halt suddenly in front of a discarded heel of bread. As he picked up the bread we began to wonder what he could possibly be doing. He looked far too healthy and well-groomed to be a beggar. Kissing the bread, he muttered something, and carefully placed it out of the main thoroughfare on a step.

Khubz (bread) is sacred in Morocco and the man was observing one of the most basic of Muslim rites which is the true honouring of bread, the most basic and essential of foods. The Prophet ordered that bread be treated with utmost respect, so any bread found thrown away in the street must be moved out of the way of foot traffic with a short prayer.

This reverence is also seen at the table. Traditionally, bread should only be distributed by one person, usually the hostess, to avoid conflict in the house. Alternatively, wedges of bread are scattered across the table within easy reach of each guest or family member so that they are not forced to ask for more. In restaurants, diners will be given a basket of bread that is replenished as often as needed.

In a culture where eating with hands is the norm, bread is used to soak up sauces and help pick up food. In rural areas and also among poorer families, bread is often the mainstay. It is often eaten with mint tea and a few olives, or grilled and topped with fresh butter, olive oil or argan oil from the nut of the argan tree, honey, or a special mixture called **amalu**, a delicious spread of argan oil mixed with almond paste and honey (see the boxed text Argan Oil later in this chapter).

In most houses, bread is made fresh every morning. Loaves are marked with a family seal before being taken, usually by a child on the way to school, to one of the communal wood-fired ovens that abound in each rural district. The bread is baked, ready for the main midday meal. Children collect the bread on their way home from school, and the sight of happy kids skipping home with loaves wrapped in brightly coloured tea towels will provide some of your most enduring memories of Morocco.

In the countryside, each small collection of homes will build an exterior clay oven in which the bread is cooked each day.

As it is left to rise only once, Moroccan bread is quite easy to make, and most women make about three or four loaves daily, depending on the size of the household. Bread is also sold everywhere by street vendors. If a family needs more bread for any reason, then a child is sent to buy some from the mother's favoured vendor. No other will do.

Traditionally, bread is made in a circular, glazed terracotta gas'a from which it also takes its shape. Moroccan women knead the bread in the gas'a until it gains maximum elasticity, and the yeast, flours and aniseed are thoroughly blended.

Wholemeal flour, or sometimes barley mixed with unbleached flour, is usually used. White flour is, fortunately, less common, as it makes for a blander loaf. Cornmeal is often sprinkled on top of the dough, adding a pleasantly crunchy texture when cooked. The wood-fired ovens in which all Moroccan bread is baked give a characteristic smoky flavour. The bread is typically quite heavy and dense, with a doughy texture and crunchy crust. In restaurants, it is often served sliced in wedges; it can be bought everywhere in small rounds marked with a cross-shaped indentation that makes it simple to break open.

Bread for sale, Fès

Tajines

After couscous, the **tajine** (stew) is Morocco's most renowned dish. Tajine refers to a method of cooking as well as a conical-lidded pot in which the dish is prepared. Essentially, tajines are stews of meat and vegetables, sometimes with the addition of fruit and nuts, cooked very slowly over a charcoal fire.

The characteristic shape of the tajine pot's lid is one of the mysteries of Moroccan cooking. Some authorities say that the conical shape was developed to retain and circulate the heat more efficiently; others say the shape simply means that the lid is big enough to cover a generous pile of simmering food, and easy to remove with one hand.

Tajine pots can be found in any number of sizes – from small, feeding only two, through to enormous, banquet-sized vessels. They are very cheap but, once seasoned, are jealously guarded by their owners (see the boxed text Seasoning a Tajine later in this section, see also Utensils in the Home Cooking & Traditions chapter).

An essential accompaniment to the tajine is the **majmar**, which is the low, unglazed terracotta brazier holding the charcoal underneath the pot. Each tajine pot has its own majmar made exactly to size. Traditionally, tajine cooking happens at floor level, which may seem awkward for those not used to the idea, but many Moroccan women cook only in this way. Nowadays however, tajines are sometimes cooked on gas in heavy saucepans or even pressure cookers, which are found in all relatively modern kitchens (see Moroccan Kitchens in the Home Cooking & Traditions chapter). For those who want to mix old with new, a well-seasoned terracotta tajine can be used with a heat-diffusing mat over a gas flame.

Methods of preparation vary. In some regions meat is marinated and sealed before adding water. It is also sometimes rubbed with herbs and spices before cooking, allowing it to absorb a variety of flavours.

In Fès ingredients are never fried first, which gives Fès-style tajines their paler colour and more delicate flavour. However they are prepared, all ingredients then cook very slowly in water which gradually becomes a rich stock. The stock eventually becomes the sauce in which the tajine is served (see Sauces later in this chapter).

Typical tajine combinations include: lamb with dates; lamb with sweetened tomatoes and almonds; lamb or chicken with preserved lemons and olives; chicken **qadra** (chicken tajine cooked in a stock of onions, smen and saffron) with chickpeas; meatballs, tomatoes and eggs; lamb with okra and tomatoes; fish with tomatoes, capsicums and green olives; and fish with celery. Variations on these and other combinations abound. One Berber tajine uses only lentils and vegetables for a nourishing, simple stew.

The secret to any good tajine is long, slow cooking and careful melding of flavours. They are generally eaten with bread, as a main course. At a banquet, you're likely to be served a variety of tajines. The classic combinations of sweet and sour flavours – with vegetables, fruits, nuts, fragrant herbs and spices, used to counterpoint the rich flavours of the meats – are testament to the medieval roots of this method of cooking, when meat was often combined with sweet elements.

Mruziyya (Lamb Tajine with Raisins & Almonds)

This dish is traditionally prepared for **Aid el Kebir** (the festival of the sacrifice of the lamb, see the Celebrating with Food chapter). Because of the over-supply of lamb at this time, the cooking of the meat in spices, butter and honey means that it keeps well and can be eaten over a number of days. The famous Moroccan spice mixture, **ras-el-hanut** (literally, shopkeeper's choice) is a prominent taste in this dish, but if you find it too fragrant, a mixture of cinnamon and ginger with a touch of black pepper will suffice (see **Ras-el-hanut** in Spices later in this chapter).

Ingredients

1kg lamb cut into pieces
salt to taste
3-4 teaspoons ras-el-hanut
1 pinch powdered saffron strands
1 stick cinnamon
200g unsalted butter
1 tablespoon olive oil
2 tablespoons honey
250g raisins
200g blanched almonds

Rub ras-el-hanut into the meat pieces and put the meat, saffron, cinnamon stick, butter and oil into a pot. Add water to cover.

Bring to the boil and simmer for about 90 minutes. Check from time to time that there is enough water to keep the meat from sticking to the pan.

Add raisins and honey. Cook for another 20-30 minutes or until the sauce is reduced to a rich syrup. Brush the blanched almonds with butter or oil and grill them until slightly browned. Before serving, sprinkle the almonds over the tajine. Serve piled onto a shallow dish.

This dish can keep for a few days if you put it into a terracotta or glass receptacle. Make sure that the meat is well covered with sauce, which will form a protective layer once it cools.

Serves 4-6 people

Djej Msharmal (Chicken Tajine with Lemon & Olives)

Ingredients

1½kg	chicken, cut into pieces (some may prefer to leave it whole)
2	chicken livers
1	teaspoon coarse salt
2	cloves garlic
1	small bunch coriander
1	large onion, peeled and grated
2	preserved lemons, peel only, rinsed and cut into strips (see boxed text Preserved Lemons later in this chapter)
1	teaspoon ground ginger
1	teaspoon ground black pepper
¼	teaspoon powdered saffron threads
4	tablespoons olive oil
2	tablespoons butter

The day before cooking, pound the salt and garlic together to make a paste. Rub the paste over the chicken and then rinse.

Combine the ginger, pulp of lemon and oil. Rub it over the chicken and leave to marinate in the fridge, covered, overnight. (If you don't have a fridge, just rub the salt and garlic paste into the chicken, rinse it, and place it in a pot with all the spices, herbs and onion.)

Place the chicken and livers in a pot with the onions, saffron and coriander and cover with water. Bring to the boil and simmer for about an hour. Remove and mash the livers, then return them to the sauce.

Add the preserved lemon peel and olives (which you may pit if you want) and let the chicken cook for a further 15 minutes or so.

Transfer the chicken to a serving platter and keep warm. Reduce the sauce by boiling until it is a thick gravy. Remove the coriander sprigs and pour the sauce over the chicken. Decorate with lemon peel and olives.

Serves 4 people

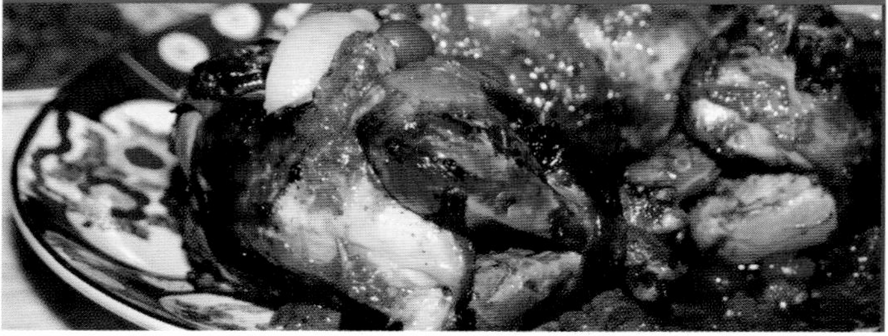

Seasoning a Tajine

If you decide to buy a terracotta tajine pot to take home with you, it is essential to season the pot before you cook with it. This is especially important if you intend to use it on a gas stove.

Place a number of your favourite vegetables (peeled) in the tajine and cover them with water.

Add olive oil, herbs and spices, chosen according to the sort of flavours you would like to impregnate the terracotta with. The classic combination of cumin, coriander, ginger and paprika is a suitable mix.

Place the tajine, covered, into a slow oven (150°C) and cook for about 40 minutes. Let the tajine cool gradually at room temperature. Remove the ingredients and wash the pot. It is now ready for use. Remember to always use a heat diffuser when cooking on a gas flame.

Another method is to bake grated onion, salt and pepper in the tajine until the ingredients turn black. This method of seasoning is used by Berbers in the Rif mountains for their regional version of the tajine, known as the **taghra**.

Sauces

Moroccan cooking is based on casseroles or stews, where all the ingredients cook together. Sauces, in the classic French sense – a separate and added component – do not exist in Moroccan cooking, which relies on the reduction of the liquid ingredients into an unctuous stock. We speak of a couscous or tajine's 'sauce' but it is in actual fact the rich stock created by the cooking process.

There are four basic stocks, or sauces, in the Moroccan repertoire, and these stocks are really the basis of the entire Moroccan culinary pantheon. Most recipes are based on the use of one or other of these stocks. To understand how to prepare each is to understand the nature of Moroccan food. Moroccan cooks vary the ingredients to achieve their own distinct signature dishes.

BASIC STOCKS

The four Moroccan stocks are:

Mqalli	a yellow sauce based on saffron and oil with ginger.
Mhammar	a red sauce based on paprika, cumin and butter.
Qadra	smen with vegetables, chickpeas and almonds.
Msharmal	a sauce of saffron, ginger and pepper.

To further simplify, Moroccan sauces are either yellow (with the addition of saffron) or red (with paprika). Whether meat, poultry, fish or vegetables are being cooked these bases remain the same. By looking for the name of the dish according to the four different stocks described above, you'll generally know what to expect. As with all Moroccan food, variations on these stocks abound. An example can be found in couscous which is usually served in what is, loosely, a qadra sauce. Some cooks choose to mix red with yellow by adding paprika to the couscous stock. This is frowned upon by some of the more 'classical' cooks, who believe paprika is too heavy with couscous. However, some accomplished cooks think the subtle aroma of paprika adds a richer dimension.

Moroccans also use a distinctive marinade, called **sharmoola**. This marinade is mainly used for fish and often as a marinade for cracked green olives. It's also used with poultry and meat.

At base, sharmoola is a mixture of parsley and coriander leaves, onion and a variety of spices including garlic, hot red pepper, sweet paprika, cumin and sometimes saffron and ginger. These ingredients are blended with olive oil, lemon juice and salt. Sometimes preserved lemons are chopped roughly through the mixture.

To prepare fish with sharmoola, cooks rub the marinade into the fish at least a half an hour before serving (as with most marinades, the longer it is left, the stronger the flavour). Once marinated, the fish is either fried (usually after being rolled in flour) or cooked slowly in a tajine.

Another sauce, mainly used as a condiment, is **harissa**, made from pulverised chillies, garlic, salt and olive oil. Harissa is not generically Moroccan, but nevertheless is often found accompanying tajines and couscous. Imported from the cuisine of Tunisia, it sits comfortably with most North African food. Moroccans often flavour harissa with a dash of cumin and coriander. It's sometimes used to lift the flavour of a grated tomato sauce which often accompanies the **brochettes** (kebabs) sold by street vendors. Some cooks also like to add a dash of harissa exuberance to couscous or any yellow stocks.

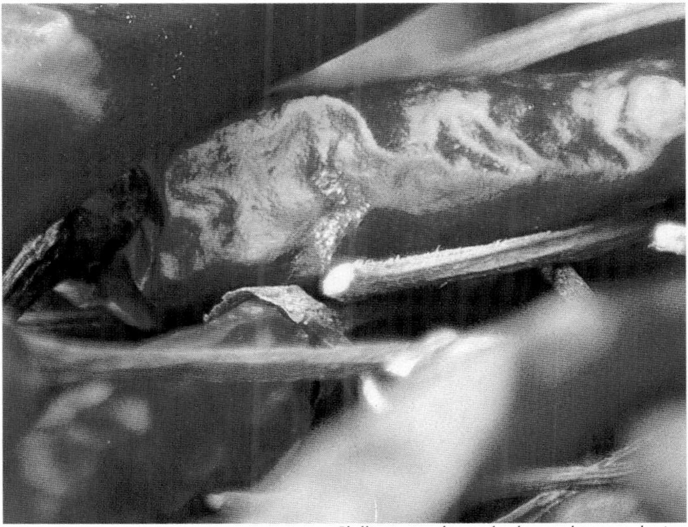

Chillies are used to make the popular sauce, harissa

Vegetables

While the imperial and banquet dishes make little use of them, vegetables abound in domestic cuisine. In mountainous areas, local vegetables may form the basis of tajines, with a little of whatever meat is available. In the richer coastal regions and in cities, fish and meat are usually the central ingredients, offset by a few choice vegetables showcasing the best of the seasonal produce. Vegetables such as potatoes, onions, cauliflowers, turnips, eggplants, radishes, capsicums, tomatoes, artichokes, okra, zucchinis, carrots, beans and broccoli grow prolifically along the broad coastal plain that stretches along the northern length of Morocco. Pumpkins and gourds are grown throughout the south.

Another renowned vegetable delicacy – one of the only imperial dishes which celebrate vegetables – is the famous **kseksu bidawi** (couscous with seven vegetables). Some vegetables, such as the thorny wild artichoke, are regarded as great delicacies. The wild artichoke grows prolifically around Fès, where it is prepared with great patience. It's said only Fassi women have enough patience and finesse to prepare it, while Casablancan women are said to be too independent and impatient to wrestle with it merely for the sake of pleasing their men.

Couscous with kseksu bidawi is one of the few imperial dishes in which vegetables are celebrated. This traditional Fassi dish plays on the number seven – seven vegetables and preferably seven spices – which Arabs regard as lucky.

Vegetables such as tomatoes and eggplants feature brilliantly in the cooked salads which grace the table before and alongside the main meal (see Salads later in this chapter).

Morocco is still primarily an agricultural society. The sector employs almost half the population and produces nearly 20% of the GDP. Of the estimated 71 million hectares of Moroccan land, 40 million are devoted to agricultural produce for both the domestic markets and for export to the European Union. Because of its warm climate, fruit and vegetables ripen sooner in Morocco, giving their exports a competitive edge.

Red capsicum

Salads

Moroccan salads are inspired combinations of cooked vegetables with an exquisite balance of flavours, enhanced by herbs and spices in the characteristic Moroccan fashion. These salads, akin to Italian antipasto, are eaten with generous quantities of bread.

Salads are served before a tajine or couscous and are often left on the table surrounding the central plate so diners can continue to eat them during the main meal.

To prepare these salads, vegetables are cooked together with spices and preserved lemons or olives, and heightened with an olive oil dressing spiked with salt, pepper and lemon juice. Cooked vegetable salads you may see include eggplant with tomato, zucchinis or capsicums and tomato, artichoke hearts and asparagus, grated beetroot with cinnamon and parsley. Preserved lemon is sometimes chopped and folded through to add flavour.

Salads can be further enhanced in a number of ways. Raw vegetables such as shredded carrots and cucumber are sometimes added. Cucumbers are marinated in sweet vinegar and sprinkled liberally with chopped parsley, coriander and orange flower water. Some vegetables, usually eggplants, capsicums, tomatoes and onions, can be stuffed with a combination of herbs, spices and breadcrumbs, and served hot or cold. Okra, at times unappetising, is delicious served with a fresh tomato sauce dip. Pulses such as chickpeas, broad beans and lentils are often served cooked in a tomato sauce or sharmoola-style sauce.

Salads and tajine

Eggplant is a favourite in Morocco, served with almost every salad accompanied by onions, tomatoes, zucchinis, or peppers. Fried in rounds, they are sold frequently at roadside stalls.

Lambs' brains and liver, cooked with spices and herbs, are also common additions to salad. Oranges are frequently served, also, flavoured with rosewater or dressed with dates or walnuts.

GARLIC

Moroccan garlic is small and pink, with a sweeter, more fragrant perfume than its European counterpart. Grated rather than chopped into dishes, Moroccan garlic can also be pulverised with a mortar and pestle and mixed with salt into a paste. Cooks often rub this paste into poultry flesh and then rinse it off before cooking. Garlic is used in most salads and often in tajines, highlighting the delicate fragrance of coriander, cinnamon and cumin with its warm aroma.

Garlic may be the only ingredient used with such enthusiasm in Moroccan cooking to have been avoided by Mohammed. Apparently he refused a dish containing garlic by explaining that he had to keep close proximity with many people.

Fruit

Because of its warm climate, Morocco is a fruit-lover's paradise. Moroccan farmers excel in the production of citrus fruit, almost half of which is exported. Different varieties of oranges, lemons and grapefruits are grown almost all year round and improved irrigation systems, including the building of dams and waterways, have boosted production.

Dates, melons, olives, plums, peaches, apricots, apples, quinces, pomegranates, figs and grapes supplement the sometimes frugal diet of much of Morocco's population. Fruits – both fresh and dried – find their way into many tajines, and are always served at the end of a meal. Bitter oranges, in particular, are used in preserving techniques.

Possibly because of the abundance of fruit, the Moroccan culinary tradition does not include a great number of desserts. Fruit is usually served providing refreshing contrast to the richness of the main meal. Sometimes, fruits are stewed lightly and served in their juices, but are more often served cut on a plate, or even whole, in a cornucopia of the season's harvest.

Pomegranates

The inclusion of fruit in meat and fish tajines and couscous dishes probably dates from the Middle Ages. The marrying of meats, fruit – often dried – and nuts was common by the time of the caliphs in the 10th century, who probably inherited it from the court cooking of the Persians. In mountainous and desert regions of Morocco, vegetables have often been in short supply, whereas fruits – especially dates, plums and quinces – are abundant. The inclusion of meat and fruit in the same dish, a tradition ironically reaching its zenith in the rich court kitchens of the rulers of the country – is ideally suited to the means of poorer rural families.

Plums

DATES

In a nomadic culture spawned in the desert, it is not surprising that the date has become something of a sacred fruit. Highly nutritious, delectably sweet, easy to harvest and transport, the date was the staple food of the Arab Islamic warriors who swept into North Africa, just as it sustained Berber and Saharan tribesmen. Originating in the fertile plains of Mesopotamia, the date palm was easily exported to the Maghreb and now flourishes all over Morocco. The country boasts many hectares of **palmeraie** (palm groves) which are particularly spectacular across the High Atlas mountains in the gorges of the Dades, Draa and Todra in the Tafilelt region. Plantations are now found all over Morocco, including the renowned palmeraie of Marrakesh.

There are over 30 sorts of date in Morocco, categorised according to weight, juiciness, size and shape. Size isn't everything, and some of the smaller ones are sweeter and more succulent. A dried date contains, by weight, over 50% sugar, and 2% each of protein, fat and minerals – so a few dates go a long way in dietary terms.

The date is religiously significant, as it is eaten with **hrira** (thick soup) to break the fast during Ramadan. In Berber areas, dates and a heel of bread may be the only accompaniments to a mint tea break. Children are given dates for **Mouloud** (Mohammed's birthday) and also to celebrate the end of Ramadan.

Dates are used in dishes such as tajines with lamb or beef, where they sweeten the rich meat flavour as well as adding a pleasing sticky texture. In medieval times, dates were thought to offset the taste of the fatty mutton which was widely used. Dates are also often used in stuffings. A celebrated Moroccan fish recipe from Fès, **hut bu-etob**, involves stuffing dates with almonds and spices, and then stuffing a fish with the dates and baking it. The fish used is the **alose** (shad), found in the Sebou river near Fès.

Preserves

Preserves are one of the cornerstones of Moroccan food. Jewish Moroccans developed preserving to an artform. Jewish quarters in Moroccan towns are called **mellah**, meaning 'salt'. It is said, perhaps unkindly, that this came about because it was the grisly task of the Jewish community (who were under the protection of, and thus obliged to, the ruling sultan) to salt and thus semi-preserve the heads of executed prisoners for display on the town walls. We'd prefer to think that the name pays homage to the Jewish skill in preserving food. There is no doubt that the addition of preserved ingredients creates some of the defining flavours in Moroccan cuisine.

You'll no doubt taste preserved lemons in tajines and salads. The lemons impart their characteristic sharp tang and silky texture to the rich sweetness of many dishes. The lemons used for preserving should be thin-skinned, small and sweet, known as **doqq** or **busera** (see boxed text on the next page). Many families preserve quantities of lemons for use throughout the year, and supplement their reserves at the **souq** (market) where preserved lemons are displayed decoratively patterned, glistening and yellow.

Olives are also commonly preserved, and eaten on their own or added to tajines. Olive trees grow prodigiously in Morocco and co-operative crushing facilities exist throughout the countryside. Most of them are simple buildings housing a huge circular mill stone which is slowly kept grinding by a stoic, plodding donkey. The two main oil-producing regions are the area bounded by Fès, Meknès and Taza (strong and hard in taste); and the area around Marrakesh (smoother). Moroccans use the raw oil in salads and vegetable dishes, preferring sunflower oil or what they call 'salad oil' for cooking tajines and couscous.

Capsicums are often preserved in a mixture of salted water and vinegar for use in tajines.

ARGAN OIL

The oil from the nut of the argan tree, grown prolifically in the south of Morocco, is highly prized.

Rarely used for cooking, Argan oil is popular in the south where it is spread on bread or pancakes or mixed with almond paste and honey to make **amalu**, a delicious spread. Sometimes a small dish is placed on the table with the salads, for dipping bread. The taste is smoother and more subtle than olive oil. Good argan oil is a lovely honey amber colour with a gentle nutty scent.

Women often use argan oil cosmetically – it is said to improve oily complexions and encourage tanning.

Preserving

Moroccan olives are among the best of all the Mediterranean countries. To experience the extraordinary variety of olives and their preparations, you need only stroll through the **souq** (market) of any large town. Olives are heaped in every colour and size, and flavoured with a wide range of condiments such as paprika, chilli, cumin, coriander and salt. Meknès, with its rich and fertile hinterland, boasts the best displays.

Olives are never eaten raw, as anyone who has tried an olive picked straight from the tree will testify. They are horribly bitter. Olives are like wine – tastes need to be slowly coaxed out of the fruit through refinement. As with wine, there are a number of colours and tastes depending on region and preparation. Size, fruitiness, pip-to-flesh ratio and flavour depend on the age of the tree, where it is grown and the condition of the soil.

Before preserving, olives are sorted according to their colour, which corresponds to their degree of ripeness, and the way in which they will be treated. Green or very young olives are cracked with a stone in such a way that only the skin is broken, leaving the pip intact. They are then soaked in brine for three to seven days, the brine being replaced at least once daily. This rids the olives of their bitterness. Following this the olives are covered with fresh water, to which lemon juice is sometimes added. Note that green olives are sold bottled in brine and should be rinsed and boiled before eating or cooking to remove bitterness.

Violet or ripe olives (violet covers a number of hues from pale tan to deep red) are traditionally treated with the juice of **laranj** (bitter oranges). Olives should be slit on one side to the depth of the pip, then washed and sealed in a glass or terracotta jar, covered with water, and left for one month. The water should then be changed, and the receptacle resealed for another 10 days. At the end of this period, the water is discarded and the **laranj** juice – which should have been bought 40 days before the olives – is mixed in, and salt added. After five days, the olives are ready for eating.

Black or very ripe olives are often pressed and dried, giving them a shrivelled appearance which is more than made up for by their sweet taste and juicy texture. These olives are pressed in a basket under heavy rocks. Initially they are left for five days. They are then laid out in the sun to dry for a day, before being re-pressed for a further five days. This operation is repeated three times. Finally, the olives are laid out in the sun for two days, and coated with peanut oil, which adds a pleasing taste and preserves the texture. Then they can be eaten. They should be kept, tightly pressed together, in a well-sealed jar.

You will often see black olives dressed in harissa, which gives a fiery, slightly bitter edge to the smooth sweetness of the olives.

Preserving Lemons

Lemons are preserved in the Moroccan spring when they are at their ripest and sweetest, and providing that the process is followed meticulously, they are quite easy to prepare.

The lemons should be washed thoroughly, and if the skins are thick, left to soak in water for up to three days. Each lemon should be cut into quarters but not all the way through, so that the quarters remain joined at the base of the fruit. Stuff salt into the interior and squeeze together. Put them into a sterilised glass or terracotta jar and push down to release some of the juice. Fill the jar with water so that all the lemons are covered and seal the jar. They can be used after one month.

Don't worry if the lemons develop a stringy, white substance, it's harmless. Remove the lemons from the jar with a wooden spoon and rinse before cooking. Usually only the rind is used, but some cooks like to use the pulp – removing the pips first – for extra flavour.

Some cooks – especially from the region around Safi – add cinnamon sticks, cloves and coriander seeds for a slightly different taste.

Preserved fruit and olives

Meats

Meat is an integral part of the Moroccan diet but assumes greatest importance at banquets, when meat and poultry dishes take centre stage. This is because meat is so much more expensive and so the host, by offering a range of meat, shows deference to his guests.

Lamb or mutton are the mainstays but beef is being used frequently these days. Kid is sometimes served on special occasions, and regarded as a great delicacy. In Saharan regions, camel is sometimes found, but this is rare, the camel being more useful as a beast of burden. Recipes for the various types of meat are interchangeable.

Lamb or mutton remains the most common meat. Sheep have been kept for centuries throughout the Arab world for the sole purpose of producing meat and, to a lesser extent, milk. It is very common for families to buy a sheep and fatten it in the home for some days before killing it. This custom is particularly evident just before **Aid el Kebhir** (festival of the sacrifice of the lamb), which takes place 50 days after Ramadan and is one of the major festivals of the Muslim calendar (see the Celebrating with Food chapter).

KEBABS

Meat **kebabs** can be found all over Morocco and are one of the most common street foods on offer.

You'll find **kefta** kebabs at almost every roadside stall. Kefta balls are formed from finely minced lamb which is mixed with spices (cumin, paprika, onion, salt and pepper, parsley and sometimes coriander) and moulded into small, sausage-shaped balls, threaded end to end and grilled. Kefta balls are also used to make the famous kefta tajine, **kefta mgawara**, which is served with tomato and eggs.

Cubes of lamb are often alternated with cubes of fat to help the meat brown and sizzle. These lamb kebabs are known by their French name, **brochette**.

Kwah (liver kebabs) are traditional accompaniments to **mashwi** (barbecued lamb) which is reserved for special occasions. Many kebab vendors sell them all year round. In this case, the fresh liver is washed, cubed, rubbed with cumin, paprika and salt and wrapped with sheep's caul or mutton fat before being grilled.

All kebabs are served enveloped between the wings of a generous serving of bread and a choice of sauces, most commonly **harissa** (hot chilli sauce). The sandwich is then topped off with a sprinkling of salt and cumin.

HALAL BUTCHERING

Muslims are particular about the way in which their beasts are slaughtered. This is called hallal butchering. The beast is pointed towards Mecca. The butcher then takes a knife, and uttering "**Bismillah**" (in the name of Allah), he cuts swiftly through the animal's throat, severing arteries and windpipe. The butcher should be a devout Muslim, who prays five times a day as decreed.

Khli' is made by marinating and drying strips of meat, particularly beef, which are then cooked and kept under a layer of fat, to be eaten throughout the year. Coarse salt is rubbed into the flesh before marinating, usually in some sort of sharmoola (see Sauces earlier in this chapter). The meat should be left in the sharmoola (or covered with a garlic and spice paste) for at least 24 hours. The meat strips are then hung out to dry, and brought in each evening to avoid any moisture. The strength of the marinade is said to keep flies at bay but a sheet of muslin is usually hung over the meat for good measure.

For the preservation to be successful, the meat must be totally dry which can take up to 10 days depending on the weather. Once dried, the meat is simmered in fat, oil, the marinade and water, until all the water evaporates and the richly flavoured fat/oil mixture is left in the bottom of the pan with the cooked meat.

Jars are then filled with layers of the meat and fat. The fat acts as a preservative to the meat. A thick plug of fat on top of the jar can be removed and replaced each time some of the khli' is used.

The meat in khli' is very strong, rich and, if well prepared, quite soft. It is used sparingly in tajines and couscous, fried with eggs and tomatoes for breakfast, or used in savoury **baghrir** or **rghayif** (pancakes).

Perhaps one of the most famous methods of preparing meat is the Berber lamb feast, **mashwi**. It is, essentially, a barbecue. A whole lamb is roasted on a spit above the glowing charcoals of a fire, built in a pit dug especially for the occasion.

The cleaned lamb is brushed inside and out with a mixture of butter, salt, pepper, cumin and sweet paprika, which is re-applied every 15 minutes or so throughout the cooking process. Cooking can take up to four hours. This method of 'dry-marinating', typical to many Moroccan grills, allows the lamb to develop a crisp golden crust while the meat inside remains delectably tender. Mashwi is accompanied by a mixture of salt and often **kwah**, (liver kebabs, see the boxed text Kebabs).

Digging a pit and roasting a whole lamb is not an activity best suited to cities, so most urban Moroccans send the beast to a community oven to be cooked. This is no substitute for mashwi cooked in the traditional way as the bakers can be inattentive. Restaurants occasionally have their own in-house clay pits where lambs are roasted and this can be an accessible way to taste mashwi. One of the best places for this is a cluster of restaurants around the abattoir in Casablanca. The mashwi is delicious – although the magnificent scent does not quite drown out the reek of slaughter nearby.

Tanzhiyya, a speciality of Marrakesh, is another meat dish that is often taken to the community oven to be cooked. It is favoured by single men because it's easy to prepare and doesn't require a stove. Tanzhiyya is named after the round-bellied pot in which it is prepared. The belly rises into a slender neck with a handle on either side. Ingredients depend entirely on the means and preferences of the cook. Meat (cuts of lamb or beef are common) and sundry seasonal vegetables are inserted through the narrow neck with water and spices. The pot is then sealed with parchment paper and string and taken to the bakery.

The tanzhiyya pots are placed in the charcoal embers of the fire. The longer the tanzhiyya takes to cook, the better the outcome; eight to 12 hours is optimum. A long, slow cooking ensures meat of melting texture, impregnated with the taste of the spices and vegetables which accompany it.

Poultry

Chicken is by far the most common meat in the Moroccan daily diet. Even in the cities, many families will keep a chicken or two in the home for easy access.

Aside from chicken, other poultry used by Moroccans includes turkeys, pigeons and quails. The latter are used almost exclusively in banquet dishes. The legendary dish, **bastila**, is usually made with chicken. (For more on bastila, see Savoury Pastries later in this chapter, and a recipe in the Moroccan Banquet chapter).

Chickens are sold live in the souqs, where they are killed and plucked (sometimes with a mechanical plucking machine rather like a giant pencil sharpener) on the spot, or taken away, flapping and complaining, to be killed at home. Their meat is often a little tough, and benefits from the long, slow cooking methods typical to Moroccan cuisine.

Chicken can be prepared in numerous ways: as part of a couscous dish, stuffed, roasted, grilled over an open fire, or boiled in a pot. Most frequently, it's cooked with an array of herbs, spices and seasonal vegetables in a tajine.

The most famous chicken tajine is **djej msharmal**, a magnificent dish which showcases the sweet/sour combination of preserved lemons and olives with onions and spices. Chicken **qadra** is also very popular, using a classic sauce of smen, vegetables and almonds, with a slash of lemon juice often added to lift the flavours.

Fruits – particularly dried – are often used in chicken tajines, sometimes in combination with almonds or chickpeas. Steamed or boiled chickens are less common, possibly because you need a really succulent bird to make a successful dish.

As a change from tajines, Moroccans like to stuff poultry, usually with rice or couscous, often mixed with almonds, cinnamon, honey or raisins; or even kefta balls and eggs.

Eggs and birds, Marrakesh

Seafood

With its long coastline bordering the Mediterranean and the Atlantic, Morocco has an abundant source of seafood. However, in a warm country where refrigerators are often considered a luxury, seafood is largely confined to the coast, its hinterland, and the Rif mountains in the north which rise from the sea. Freshwater fish can be found seasonally inland. The better restaurants in Marrakesh and, to a lesser extent, Fès are extremely conscientious about the seafood they offer.

Once again, tajines are a favourite way to prepare fish. Whole fish are laid out on a bed of bamboo stalks, celery or carrot sticks (to prevent the fish sticking to the bottom of the dish), and soused in sharmoola. Preserved lemons, olives, tomatoes, potatoes, peppers, onions and even eggs often embellish the dish.

One of the most elaborate dishes in Morocco is fish baked with stuffed fruit. Prunes or dates are stuffed with almonds and spices; the fruit is then used to stuff the cavity of a large, white-fleshed fish. Originating in Fès – the city famous for its sweetened dishes and intricate flavours – the fish is usually a freshwater variety of shad found in the Sebou River, although the same dish may be found near the coast using sea fish such as mackerel.

Fishing boats at Essaouira

Savoury Pastries

Moroccans are accomplished pastry makers. Their pastries typically follow a few broad themes which are of course open to the standard Moroccan variables of season and cook. One of the most renowned of Moroccan dishes is **bastila**. For many aficionados, a discussion of Moroccan food begins and ends with bastila, the extraordinary dish of multi-layered flaked pastry leaves, interspersed with shredded pigeon or chicken meat, moistened with a mixture of two dozen eggs gently curdled in a lemony onion sauce and studded with almonds. It is often topped with a generous layer of cinnamon and sugar.

Apart from the opposition of sweet and sour flavours and the richness of the ingredients, the outstanding feature of bastila is the **warqa** pastry used. It's said that a cook is not really a cook in Morocco until she masters the making of warqa; a skill of hand, eye, a deft touch, and above all, patience (see the boxed text Making Warqa later in this section).

Making warqa is a painstaking process. Imagine, firstly, the finest, translucent leaves of pastry. Imagine squatting for hours over a hot pan and tap-tap-tapping a ball of wet dough in unending circular patterns. Imagine the vigilance and persistence needed to produce over 40 sheets for each pie, which is about 30cm in diameter. The good warqa makers are celebrated in Morocco. Due to its complexity and the skill needed to prepare the pastry, bastila is a dish that is usually reserved for banquets or special occasions.

The warqa is prepared on the base of a **tobsil** (large, low, circular pan which is heated by upending it over a charcoal or gas flame). Often, in

PANCAKES

Pancakes, both savoury and sweet, feature highly in the national diet. A favourite breakfast food, **rghayif**, can be served sweet with honey or icing sugar, or savoury with khli' or any other type of meat. On holidays, they're often served with almond paste.

Rghayif are, basically, a type of puff pastry, fried in oil and served hot. Depending on the shape and filling, they may also be called **miklee**, **mlawi**, **mekhtamrin** or **metlouh**, rghayif being the generic name for this type of pastry. **Rghayif el mila**, made with eggs, are served at circumcision celebrations.

Baghrir pancakes have a distinctive pattern of tiny bubble pits on one side, formed as the pancake cooks. They're usually served hot with butter and honey or icing sugar.

restaurants, the warqa maker can be seen seated on a rolled carpet in the corner of the kitchen with her tobsil braced over what appears to be a bunsen burner, working away quietly with a meditative intensity. The tobsil, turned over, becomes the receptacle in which the bastila is prepared. Modern versions of bastila include the use of seafood and a sweet version oozing with a custardy milk and diced almonds (see Sweet Pastries under Sweet Dishes later in this chapter).

Some Moroccans believe that bastila originated with the first wave of Arab invaders, who brought with them the concept of encasing meat in pastry leaves. They say the Arabs got the idea from the Persians, who got it from the Chinese. Others theorise that bastila was brought back to

MAKING WARQA

As an observer and a very feeble novice, I can attest that talking about warqa is much easier than making it. In Rabat, the Royal Cooking School (*Centre de Formation en Cuisine Traditionelle*, set up by King Hassan II within the Palace complex) teaches young women how to become master cooks and one of their tasks is the making of warqa. A young apprentice, watched keenly by one of her supervisors, conscientiously patted a large glob of wet pastry on the hot pan in a rhythmic, circular pattern. The pastry solidified, rather like egg white, and was then peeled off in a smooth action. At least, that's the theory. The supervisor, a kind woman despite her eagle eye, assured me that in reality, the first few leaves of warqa never work. I was happy to let that axiom stand when it came to my turn.

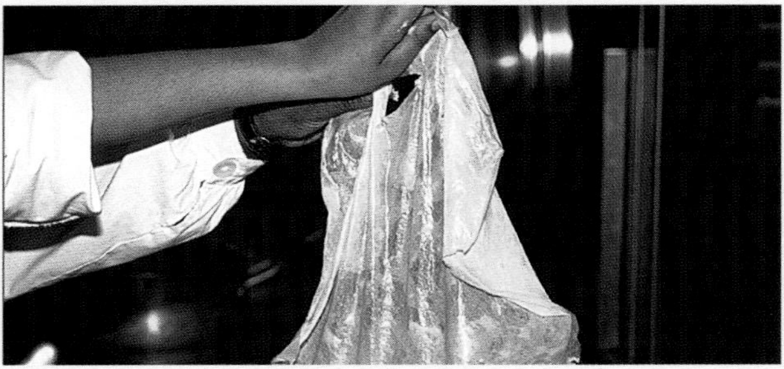

Morocco by Andalucian immigrants after the reconquista in Spain (see History in The Culture of Moroccan Cuisine chapter). One way or another, it is a dish that illustrates the meeting of many cultures in its flavours. Bastila appears more closely related in texture and preparation to the Chinese spring roll than to filo or strudel pastry. However, the traditional use of pigeons and the combination of flavours in the sauce suggest the influence of Spain. Nowadays in Morocco, southern desert women are said to be the best warqa makers.

Many women buy warqa leaves from the local expert – making them is so time-consuming and experts do the job so much better. Also, bastila is often prepared in large quantities for a banquet, the usual serving ration

MAKING WARQA

In Fès, at the marvellous boutique, hotel and restaurant, *La Maison Bleue*, I watched the warqa cook – an elegant old woman rumoured to have been the right hand chef to the King – prepare the dough and then make the leaves. Assisted by her daughter, she directed the proceedings – a little more salt, a splash more water, more energetic kneading. Then, the unpromising-looking, greyish mixture was left to sit for while. She inspected it from time to time closely, then pronounced it ready.

She positioned herself on the faded carpet, in front of an ancient tobsil and a small portable gas flame. Taking up a ball, she bounced the elastic dough in her right hand like a bunch of worry beads then touched it to the pan with authority, speed and the utmost delicacy. The supervisor at the Royal Cooking School was right – the first few leaves weren't successful. But the fourth leaf was. The dabs of gluey dough formed a seamless layer which quickly filmed over and became opaque. The warqa was cooked. Carefully, she patted the centre, flicked up the edges, and peeled off the pastry. The process was repeated time and again in a smooth rhythm.

SFENZH – MOROCCAN DOUGHNUTS

Sfenzh are best eaten hot, straight from the deep fryer. Almost every street has a sfenzh vendor, who threads his wares onto a shred of palm frond, knotted into a handle. Moroccans often eat them in the morning but they make for a reliable snack at any time of day and are especially popular with children.

being one pie for each table of six to eight guests (remember that extravagant overcatering is absolutely assured at any Moroccan party). This leaves a huge number of warqa leaves to produce, given that banquets are never small and intimate affairs.

The method of making warqa can be simplified and used for making **trid** and **briwat**, two other savoury pastry dishes found all over Morocco. Trid is often called the poor man's bastila, and has the added imprimatur of being widely accepted as the favourite food of the Prophet. Trid pastry is similar to warqa, but is fried and uses fewer leaves. However, it is not as refined as bastila and actually more time-consuming to make. Usually, fenugreek rather than the more expensive saffron is used. Trid is often served with a glass of milk.

Briwat are very small pies. Warqa pastry is folded around a variety of fillings, then baked or fried to produce delectable morsels that are served as **amuse-bouches** (snacks). They are served in any number of ways, usually as part of a larger meal. Thinking of them as finger food in the western sense, will give you an idea of their purpose.

There are two traditional shapes for briwat; triangles or cigars. Where possible, warqa pastry is used. However, as with bastila, a serviceable copy can be made with spring roll, filo or strudel pastry. If warqa or spring roll pastry is used, the briwat should be fried; filo or studel pastry should be baked. Fillings can be savoury or sweet. Savoury fillings can encompass any number of combinations – some of the most popular are fish and herbs, kefta mince, brains, rice and sometimes chicken or spinach. Interestingly, rice briwat are sweet and very often served at the beginning of the meal with mint tea.

A variant of the briwat is the Tunisian **brik**, which has been enthusiastically adopted by Moroccans. Briks are deep fried, and usually include an egg and often tuna, although any filling is deemed acceptable for a brik. Best eaten hot and straight out of the frying pan, briks in Morocco typically include a bevy of Moroccan herbs and spices – coriander, parsley, cumin, salt and pepper – and are often eaten with harissa on the side.

Pulses & Nuts

Chickpeas, lentils and couscous are the basis of many of the gastronomic marvels of Moroccan cooking. Over centuries of refinement, meat, fruit and spices were added to what were humble peasant dishes using the most basic ingredients – pulses and grains – as nourishment.

While lentils and broad beans are commonly used in Moroccan cooking, chickpeas are the most common pulse, found in everything from couscous to tajines, salads and soups. In the souqs, vendors sell little paper cones of hot chickpeas, which are eaten like popcorn.

Moroccan cooks usually peel chickpeas so that their creamy, nutty texture melds with the consistency of the stewed meats and vegetables. Lentils are used most frequently in soups, notably hrira. One Berber tajine uses lentils exclusively and they are also used to thicken some salad dishes. Like chickpeas, lentils provide an excellent foil for highly flavoured vegetables like capsicums, tomatoes and garlic.

Broad beans are used like other pulses. A Rif speciality, **bisahra**, is a thick puree of beans flavoured with cumin and paprika used as a dip or, if thinned out with water, as a soup.

The addition of nuts to enhance the flavour and texture of stews is a culinary tradition all over the Middle East, dating from the time of the Persian Empire. Almonds are often added as a garnish. Sometimes they are toasted to crispness, and scattered over the dish as a textural counterpoint; in other recipes they are cooked in the stew with the major ingredients. Almonds and walnuts are used to stuff dates and sometimes prunes, which in turn can be used to stuff poultry or fish.

The use of nuts in cooking originated in the court of the caliphs, where they indicated opulence. Bowls of nuts are often present in the home to greet visitors, or presented with fruits at the end of a meal.

nuts & seeds

Flower Water

Flower water made from bergamot flowers (bitter orange flower water) and roses is used widely in Moroccan cooking. Distilled in the **qettara** (alembic) used by the Arabs for centuries in chemistry experiments, flower water gives Moroccan preserves, drinks and sweet pastries their characteristic flavour. It is also used as a perfume – older Moroccan gentlemen apparently favour orange flower water when they are going courting.

Flower water can be found ready-made in the souqs but many Moroccan families make their own. Home made stuff tends to be much more fragrant than the bought variety.

In spring, fragrant piles of flower buds are seen in huge wicker baskets throughout the markets of Morocco. About six kilograms of flowers are required to distil about 10 litres of water. After distillation, the water should sit for about four or five months to mature before being used. Good flower water is used sparingly, otherwise it can overwhelm other ingredients.

Butter & Yoghurt

Moroccan butter inspires opinions as strong as its flavour – some people can't abide it, while others swear that it's a unique delicacy. Unique is probably the key word although we didn't find **smen** (preserved butter) nearly as awful as others have. The scent is reminiscent of a strong blue cheese and it gives many Moroccan dishes a smack of authenticity. It loses much of its pungency when mixed with other ingredients.

Similar to Indian ghee, the simplest smen is made by melting butter, straining it through a fine cheesecloth, and adding salt. Southern Moroccans spice the cooked butter with a herb found in the scrubby pre-Sahara called **zatar**, which tastes like a combination of oregano and marjoram. Oregano, marjoram and thyme are also sometimes used. The citizens of Fès and the southern Berbers share a taste for very old smen, which is kept for years in terracotta jars.

Zebda is a butter made in the spring from curdled milk. Fresh milk is left to stand for two or three days in an earthenware jug, and then churned in a **khabya** until the milk separates. Zebda is used fresh for cooking or made into smen. The remaining buttermilk, **iben**, is highly prized and drunk with sweet couscous at banquets, or at breakfast with pancakes.

An unusual Moroccan yoghurt, **rayib**, is made from milk thickened with the hairy hearts of wild Moroccan artichokes. At any time of the day you'll see people popping into **laiteries** (milk and soft-drink sellers) to indulge in this yoghurt sweetened with sugar and set individually in glasses or bowls, with a thin layer of cream settling on top. It's a delicious cheap treat at only Dr2 a serving. Imported French yoghurt is widely available.

Flowers and water, Fès,

Sweet Dishes

While desserts aren't hugely popular, they're likely to show up between the main meals of tajine or couscous and the finale of fruit. They are mostly reserved for special occasions or banquets, but can also be found in good restaurants throughout Morocco.

Seffa (sweet couscous) is made with cinnamon, sugar, and sometimes studded with prunes, raisins and almonds. This dish is usually accompanied by a glass of milk or buttermilk.

Rice can be prepared in the same fashion, and rice pudding, flavoured with flower water, almonds, cinnamon and sugar is also popular.

Sweet Pastries

Consistent with the idea of mixing sweet and savoury, Moroccans often serve sweet pastries at the beginning of a meal. This tradition is usually only followed in the home these days as restaurants cater almost exclusively to foreigners who don't expect a sweet pastry as an aperitif.

Sweet pastries are also served for morning and afternoon tea, and less often for dessert. As desserts, they may be served more to replicate what Moroccans understand of western-style eating, rather than any Moroccan tradition. You may find yourself the only person eating, while your hosts ply you with a pile of the sweet pastries they think you are used to.

The best-known pastries are **ka'b ghzahl** (gazelles' horns or ankles, crescent-shaped pastries) best when the pastry is very thin and fresh. Fingers of fatima (cigar-shaped briwat slathered in honey) and **mhannsha** (the snake, a large coil of pastry dusted with icing sugar). All are filled with almond paste or pounded date and fig and scented with orange flower water.

Moroccans also make a range of biscuits, the most popular of which are called **faqqas** and **krachel**. Flavoured with aniseed and sesame seeds, or almonds and raisins, these hard little biscuits are excellent taken with mint tea. **Ghriyyba**, a type of macaroon made with semolina flour, is also found in all decent **patisseries** (pastry shops).

Honeyed cakes are served at feasts and religious festivals. **Shabbakiya** (a honeyed cake made in the shape of a rosette) is eaten traditionally with **hrira** soup at Ramadan. **Sellu**, a cone of grilled flour, sesame seeds, almonds and cinnamon doused with a honey and butter sauce, is often served at birth parties and weddings.

A variation of bastila often served at banquets uses the same technique of layered warqa pastry but is interspersed with cinnamon and almonds. Called **keneffa**, this dessert is rich, messy and sublimely delicious. It is served in a large round cake, cut in slices to reveal the rich layers. It is often served with a glass of almond milk.

Sweet meats, Moroccan style

Herbs & Spices

Spices were first brought to the Maghreb by the Arabs, who were ideally placed on the spice route between east and west and who were to become the middlemen in this fiercely contested trade. Other spices came with the caravans trading across the Sahara from Senegal.

Spices were used in Europe to enliven the porridges, and often to disguise the nature of meat which was frequently heavily salted and less than fresh. Moroccan court chefs, like those in Europe and the near East, experimented with the use of spices in their cuisine, reworking native dishes, as well as introducing dishes from the kitchens of Persia. The result was a magnificently fragrant array of dishes that were at their most elaborate in court banquets but also adopted in the tajines, couscous and sweet dishes of the people.

Spice display, Fès

In Morocco, the Arabs planted saffron, citrus fruit and almond trees. They imported a plethora of spices including cinnamon, pepper, ginger, turmeric and gum arabic as well as the spicy vegetables, garlic and onion. To this potent mix the Moroccans themselves added coriander – usually used in leaf form – parsley and cumin, all of which are native to the Mediterranean region.

The spice **souqs** (markets) in the towns show the great and colourful variety of spices used in the everyday cooking of Moroccans. Bright red paprika and cayenne peppers, soft-hued ginger, yellow turmeric, dusty sticks of cinnamon, pale seeds of cumin and greenish seeds of aniseed are heaped in great tubs to be measured out into hand-twisted envelopes of paper. Bunches of fresh coriander and parsley can be found garnishing vegetables at most of the fruit and vegetable vendors, although many Moroccans have their own small home-grown plots of these herbs next to the ubiquitous mint. Ground spices do not keep well over a long period of time, so Moroccan cooks usually only buy small quantities and keep them in airtight jars.

Following is a description of the most commonly used herbs and spices which are used in both savoury and sweet Moroccan recipes.

Mint trolley in Fès

Qarfa (Cinnamon)

Mostly used in stick form, there are two types of cinnamon available: Ceylonese which is pale and light in taste; and **cassia**, which is dark and strong in taste. Cinnamon is used throughout Moroccan cooking in soups, tajines, salads, bastila and sweets. The quantity varies, but the flavour of cinnamon is an enduring theme.

Kahmoon (Cumin)

Another of the primary tastes in Moroccan food. Cumin is native to the Mediterranean basin and in seed form looks unprepossessing and smells a bit like hay. When crushed, however, the delicious aroma and taste are released. Used to coat roast meats, it is also often tasted in tajines, notably in the company of fish and chicken.

Qesbur (Coriander)

Used in great quantities. Like parsley, Moroccan cooks buy coriander in bulk and freeze it, ready-diced, in large plastic bags. The leaves are commonly used and sometimes the seeds, although seed coriander is more a tradition on the other side of the Mediterranean. Seed coriander is used with cumin to flavour roast meats.

Madnus (Parsley)

The flat-leafed variety is used in Morocco. It's a common ingredient, almost always used in partnership with coriander.

Zafaran (Saffron)
Taken and planted by the Arabs all over the Mediterranean basin, saffron should be prepared from the pulverised stamens of crocus flowers which were traditionally collected by Moroccan Jews. It is expensive to buy and only relatively small quantities are used as it is potent in both colour and taste. Saffron is the basis of a family of Moroccan sauces.

Qarqub (Turmeric)
Often used to supplement saffron when extra colour or flavour is required, but is not really a substitute, having a coarser flavour and finish than saffron.

Skeen Zhbeer (Ginger)
Always used in the powdered variety, ginger originated in southern China and is often seen in Moroccan cooking with black pepper and coarse salt.

Falfla Khal (Black Pepper)
Used in most savoury dishes.

Ssudahniya (Cayenne)
Cayenne is used to spice a dish, and is especially favoured in tajines. Used more frequently in the south, where the influence of Senegalese cooking (which favours hotter, spicier dishes) is stronger.

Falfla Hamra (Paprika)
Paprika is the most commonly used of the pepper condiments and is the basis for many sauces. Beware of false paprika, which is often coloured with cochineal by vendors. Demand to smell and taste before you buy.

Halba (Fenugreek)
Said by the Berbers to make a woman alluringly plump, fenugreek seeds are sometimes used in Berber bread.

Anissun (Aniseed)
Often used in seed form to flavour Moroccan bread, sweets and milk drinks. Sometimes used in small quantities in tajines.

Ras-el-hanut (Mixed Spices)

Literally translated as 'shopkeeper's choice' ras-el-hanut is a special mixture of spices that is often used in Moroccan food, notably in **mruziyya** lamb and some game dishes. Made up of a special mixture of many spices (the amount and relative quantities are precisions known only to each maker), ras-el-hanut is like the signature fragrance of a perfumer – it has an artful and characteristic scent and no two are alike. Generally speaking however, the mixture contains about 13 ingredients including all the spices mentioned above, as well as lavender, thyme, mace, cardamom, and rosebuds. Ras-el-hanut is said to be good for an upset stomach.

drinks

Water has often been scarce or undrinkable in Morocco. Consequently beverages here are carefully prepared and seldom swigged. Tea drinking is elevated to a refined art – the sweet fragrance of freshly-brewed **na'na'** (mint) tea will be one of the most evocative memories of any visit. Almond milk is synonymous with celebration and ordinary fruit juice becomes delectable with the addition of a few drops of orange flower-scented water.

Cristal

Mint Tea

Many Moroccans will tell you that tea has been a part of their culture since time immemorial. It's said that Moroccans drink so much tea because it was the favoured drink of the Prophet, who decreed it take a central, ritual place in decent Moroccan society.

The Prophet is responsible for many good things in Morocco, but tea isn't one of them. In fact, the British introduced it in the mid nineteenth century. It must have fulfilled a gustatory gap because it was embraced with alacrity and, these days, some Moroccans drink nothing else. As a mark of its importance, a ritualised ceremony has evolved around the offering and drinking of tea, a ceremony which bears all the hallmarks of the Arabic tradition of hospitality.

Moroccan tea is always deeply infused with **na'na'** (mint), the fragrance of which is one of the essential elements of the heady, spiced scent of the Moroccan culinary experience.

The bracing effects and flavour of tea married well with the existing local tradition of mint **tisane**, an infusion of mint leaves in boiling water. Moroccans absorbed the foreign ingredient into their own culture transforming it into the ceremony that has become central to Moroccan society today. In the **medina** (old quarter) of all Moroccan towns and cities, the complex weave of scents, both fair and foul, is threaded with the seductive, invigorating aroma of endlessly brewing mint tea.

History

The British may have cast an envious eye on the riches of Morocco from time to time, but the most enduring foothold that they made in the country was the introduction of tea. It was an inspired piece of marketing, born out of desperation and an oversupply of a valued commodity.

In 1854, British merchants, frustrated by the blockades imposed as a result of the Crimean War, decided to offload the tea that they had collected in the Far East at the ports of Tangier and Mogador (now Agadir). A new, voracious market was born. To this day, the green tea used in making the Moroccan mint – gun powder, or *chun mee* – is the most Chinese of teas. Packets of tea can be bought in any town at any corner **epicerie** (general store) or **hypermarche** (huge supermarket).

Preparation

Chinese tea is only the beginning of the process. The preparation of the brew requires three other staples: mint, sugar and boiling water. It begins with rinsing the teapot with boiling water. This washes away any residue while warming the pot. Add tea to the pot and pour boiling water on top.

Mint trolley, Fès

Let it brew for a minute or so. Then, add a handful of mint, which should be stuffed firmly down inside the pot. Add sugar, broken from the white sugar cones that Moroccans prefer (sugar cubes and loose sugar apparently make for a different and inferior taste). The mixture should be left to sit for three minutes or so and then stirred lightly.

Of course there are infinite variables. Firstly, the tea can be of varying strength. Some Moroccans make their mint tea quite fortifying, with a good dose of tea leaves. Others prefer less tea, and more mint and sugar. Having said this, the only time we ever came across weakly minted tea was when trapped in a rug trader's den in a Marrakesh souq. A glass was thrust into our reluctant hands as a prelude to the bargaining we had no intention of pursuing. The tea tasted bad enough to put a first-time sipper off for good (which, luckily, we weren't – just weak shoppers). We learnt two rules of thumb about being politely firm in souqs. Firstly, refuse tea unless you're seriously considering buying something. Secondly, if the tea is really bad, then beware of the goods you're bargaining for.

They put a lot of sugar in Moroccan mint tea, so if you don't like very sweet tea, ask that less sugar be added. Moroccans will usually ask your preference before brewing but if you want to do as the locals do, take yours very sweet and very strong.

TRADITIONAL TEA MAKING UTENSILS

There are a number of traditional utensils that are always used for tea making in Morocco.

Siniyya – low round tray on legs in chased copper or steel. Most houses have a large one and a small one. The large one holds the teapot and glasses, the small one holds the boxes full of tea, mint and sugar.

Rbaia – cylindrical boxes holding tea, mint and sugar glasses. Tea is always served in glasses decorated with fine gold or transparent colours. For ordinary occasions, the glasses are undecorated.

Barrahd – teapot with a pointed top, usually made of stainless steel, silver or aluminum.

Bahbur – these ornate, magnificent samovars are mainly seen in hotels nowadays. In the 19th century, they were used by wealthy houses and the courts to serve boiling water for tea. Bahburs came from Russia via England, and brought these samovars with them. The intricate decoration appealed to the Moroccan sense of opulence, and samovars were very popular for a while.

Tea is often heavily sugared in the countryside, probably because it's usually accompanied by a heel of bread and a few olives at break time, and the sugar provides an energy boost. Tea in Fès, for example, is seen as a more refined accompaniment to a social and gastronomic occasion. If rich and/or fatty foods are being served, then the tea is likely to be less sugared so that it will act as a **digestif** (aid to digestion) to the meal.

Sugar cones are readily available at epiceries, although most Moroccans who have access to the increasing number of hypermarches that are beginning to tag onto the outskirts of major towns and cities, will buy them there in bulk. Sugar cones are dense, highly refined and highly prized. They are given by dinner or wedding guests as gifts to their hosts. Sugar in Morocco has a high and esteemed profile and even looks regal. The sugar cones are usually wrapped in thin paper of imperial purple (some of the supermarkets cover them in plastic of the same colour).

The cone, broken expertly into chunks, slowly dissolves in the infusion. As with most Moroccan culinary preparations, amount depends on the liaison between eye and practised taste, although a good rule is that for each three cup pot, 25 to 30g of sugar will suffice. Adjust according to taste.

Varieties of Tea

While other teas can be bought in supermarkets in the major towns, mint tea is ubiquitous. The staple ingredients are everywhere. Every day fragrant, heavily laden carts of mint are towed in from the provinces behind tiny donkeys, to be sold in the souqs of every city, town and village (see the photograph earlier in this chapter). Mint is grown all over Morocco but flourishes in mountainous regions, where it is said that the combination of cold weather and hot sun nurtures especially good plants. Most Moroccan families who have a tiny plot of land, a garden, or even a receptacle with a few handfuls of soil and a slither of sun, will grow their own to be plucked as required. Spearmint, or *mentha spicata*, is the mint of choice.

Sometimes, other herbs or flavourings are added to give variation to the mint taste. Sage, orange flower, marjoram, verbena and absinthe are common. **Shsheeba**, the absinthe-type herb (akin to fennel) has a smoky, slightly bitter liquorice flavour. It is also used to flavour soups and tajines.

In the south, saffron is sometimes added to mint tea. Saffron, the basis of many Moroccan sauces, grows abundantly in the area around Taliouine, and when the crocus flower (from which saffron threads are harvested) is ready, saffron tea is often made. In this tea, a teaspoon of saffron threads are added to the hot water and left to brew with the mint. Sometimes the saffron is used without mint (but plenty of sugar as usual). A highly prized and expensive ingredient, not widely used.

Tea Etiquette

Tea accompanies meals and most social or business exchanges in Morocco. It can be served, on its own, or with a selection of Moroccan pastries and biscuits for morning or afternoon tea. It is served before and after meals and sometimes, but rarely, with meals. It is also recommended for upset stomachs and headaches. In the countryside, tea is often served with grilled bread and honey or **argan** oil (oil from the argan tree), and a handful of olives.

Mint tea is always served in small, decorative glasses, and is often topped with a sprig of fresh mint. It is always served from a teapot in the 'Manchester' shape, inherited directly from the British heavy-bellied form, with a conical lid. This teapot is called a **barrahd**.

The teapot is usually made of metal – in more affluent homes, the metal is silver. In tea houses, aluminium is the norm. These humble aluminium teapots can be bought in souqs for a few dirham, and many a battered teapot has made a good, bracing cup of mint tea.

When served ceremonially at a 'tea party' or before a meal, the Barrahd appears on a four legged silver tray called a **siniyya**, surrounded by **rbaia**, octagonal silver boxes, which hold the mint, sugar and tea. The hostess lifts off the intricately embroidered veil which always covers the tray when it is not in use and, sitting cross-legged in front of it, proceeds to mix the ingredients deftly. After the tea has brewed for some minutes, she stirs it once or twice, and pours a stream of fragrant liquid from a great height into one of the pretty glasses. This first glass is always examined and poured back into the pot. Then, the glasses are all filled with the same high-handed, flourishing pour, and mint is added to each.

Mint Tea

These are the suggested amounts for a small 3-4 person teapot.

1 tablespoon of green Chinese tea
a generous handful of fresh mint, with more leaves than stem
25-30g of sugar (adjust to taste)

Put all the above ingredients into a teapot that has been rinsed with boiling water. Cover ingredients with boiling water and allow to brew for three or four minutes. Stir once or twice only, then pour one glass of liquid into a glass. Return this glassful to the pot. Now pour glasses of tea and garnish with fresh mint leaves if required. Try to pour the tea into the glass from as high a point as possible (without spilling it or burning a guest) as this will 'aerate' the tea as well as allow the delicious fragrance to permeate the room.

Berber serving tea

Politeness dictates that three glasses of mint tea be taken at a tea party or the conclusion of a meal. In a restaurant, you may be given only one glass. Sipping loudly is acceptable, even taken as a sign of appreciation. Tea is not taken with a meal, as to drink too much liquid suggests that you are avoiding the food.

At a tea gathering, a selection of pastries and biscuits is offered. If you refrain from tasting whatever is on offer, your hosts will pile your plate high with delicacies – it is simply not acceptable to refuse. As a sign of appreciation, you must try everything.

Tea houses – often called cafes – abound in Morocco. Any eating establishment apart from the more formal restaurants will serve tea on its own (except perhaps at meal times, when you may find that you are expected to order food).

Sometimes tea is offered without the fanfare of the ceremony, having been prepared out of sight. Sometimes the teapot, complete with tea, mint and sugar, is put back onto a low flame (or in the country, embers of charcoal) to simmer gently for a minute before the liquid is poured. You'll see the simplest tea ceremonies performed all the time in the streets, on the side of a dirt road, or in the fields. The common elements are the battered metal teapot, the high-handed pour, the glasses, and the ginger, noisy intake of the first piping hot sips. Tea drinking is always a relaxed, communal experience. No one ever drinks tea on the run.

When you drink tea in a cafe or restaurant, it's usually served ready-made in a pot accompanied by a glass.

TO A TEA

Why did Moroccans take so enthusiastically to tea? Some hypothesise that tea is the only acceptable vice in Islamic society – alcohol and other drugs being strictly forbidden. It's also cheap (much cheaper than coffee, for example), readily available, easy to make and comforting. Mint tea fortifies and energises. Being mildly addictive, it also gives a pleasant boost to the habitual drinker. Both warm and refreshing, it is perfectly suited to a country where the climate can be both enervatingly hot and bitterly cold.

Mint is also good for the stomach and aids digestion – an obvious asset in a culture that often favours rich, highly spiced foods. Finally, it requires boiled water, which means that water of dubious quality is rendered relatively harmless.

Coffee

Coffee in Morocco is generally served *a la francais* and is best drunk espresso, without milk. The milk accompanying coffee in the standard cafes can be of dubious quality, and often has thick clots of cream or an unpleasant smell. If you like your cup thick, gritty and bitter, then Turkish-style coffee is sometimes on offer. **Cafe au lait** (coffee with milk) is best tried in private homes or five-star hotels.

Almond Milk

After mint tea, **sharbat billooz** (almond milk) is probably Morocco's best-known beverage. It is traditionally drunk at festivities and celebrations such as weddings but can sometimes be found in restaurants and cafes. Almonds are not cheap, and a considerable number are used in almond milk, hence increasing its value and status.

Almond milk is made from whole blanched almonds blended with milk, water, rosewater or orange flower water and sugar. As with all juices, it should be strained before serving, and served well-chilled. Almond milk is occasionally made with water only (this is a Spanish way), the almonds giving the beverage its characteristic cloudy colour and texture.

It is one of a group of drinks called **sharbats**, which are fruit and/or nut drinks, blended with milk and perfumed with orange flower or rose water. Apart from almonds, apples and raisins are also commonly used. While almond milk is used as the favoured drink for special occasions, other sharbats are often served as a late afternoon or early evening aperitif on hot days.

AVOCADO SMOOTHIES

If you're used to appreciating avocado for its savoury qualities, you're in for a surprise treat when you taste the popular drink l'avocat, a frothy green combo of avocado blended with milk and sugar. Popularly bought at laiteries, the rich, satisfyingly filling concoction is a meal in itself.

Margo Daly

Fruit Juices

Thanks to the climate, oranges are one of Morocco's most abundant fruits. Fresh orange juice vendors are common in the major towns, their wares piled precariously high on either side of strategically parked trolleys. The oranges are pulped in front of you, and the juice is sweet or tart depending on the season. In December, oranges are very sweet and very cheap.

Moroccans often enhance the taste by adding a touch of cinnamon, sugar or orange flower water. When the juice is sweet, a couple of drops of orange flower water lifts the taste from simple orange juice to something mysterious and delectable.

Orange flower water is added to most juices, and you'll find it with pomegranate, watermelon, grapes or strawberries, sometimes with a pinch of cinnamon. This combination is often used for a less common juice made from pulped beetroots and for carrot juice. Lemon or lime juice is diluted with water, sweetened (to taste) with sugar, and also sprinkled with orange flower water. To serve these juices in the Moroccan manner, they must always be sieved through a fine-meshed strainer before adding the condiments. All should be served well-chilled.

Soft Drinks

The only beverage as pervasive as mint tea in Morocco is Coca-Cola. The marketing of this drink is phenomenal. Even the most faded grocery stores in the tiniest villages boast a Coca-Cola sign, unmistakable even though the signature is in Arabic script. Bright red plastic crates of Coca-Cola are carried into the most inhospitable areas strapped to the backs of donkeys. Stories of Coca-Cola's power to settle an upset stomach have reached legendary proportions in Morocco. It is widely drunk at all times of the day and night, with all meals and is available in cans and bottles of varying sizes. Pepsi hasn't arrived, or perhaps isn't bothering.

Other soft drinks such as Fanta or the French brand Orangina, and various lemonades are also widely available in grocery stores, restaurants, cafes, mobile trolleys and supermarkets.

If you are particularly fastidious, remember that bottles are probably more hygienic than cans, particularly because straws are not always easy to find. Cans may have collected some unwanted microbes around the mouthpiece that will be picked up and swallowed as you swig.

Water & Mineral Water

Water in Moroccan towns is theoretically drinkable despite the taste. The provision of running, drinkable water can still be problematic. Even in a big city such as Fès, the medina has no running water, and people rely on local wells dotted throughout the city. Water in the country may be bore water so be careful. If you fear the deleterious effects of enthusiastic local stomach bugs, it's probably better to drink the local bottled mineral water – sold under two labels, **Sidi 'li** and **Sidi Hrazim** (we preferred 'li) – or the bubbly mineral water called **Oulmes**. The label on Sidi 'li proclaims it especially suitable even for babies, because it respects 'the equilibrium of each organism'. These brands of bottled water are readily available everywhere costing a few dirham for a 1.5 litre bottle.

Water sellers can be seen in souqs everywhere. They are men dressed in unmistakably bright colours with marvellous pom-pom hats, carrying highly polished copper drinking vessels, and what look like bagpipes filled with water, slung around their waists (see the photograph overleaf for an introduction). Don't be tempted by their festive, polished appearance and don't try the water unless you, literally, have the stomach for it. The pretty, chased copper water vessels are not sterilised between patrons, no matter what you are told.

As with so many other beverages in Morocco, water is often flavoured with rose or orange flower water and served chilled. It is sometimes also served with chopped mint or lemon. Another method – which is used less frequently but dates back to medieval times – is to invert a water jug over gum arabic burnt in the charcoal of a brazier. The jug is then filled with chilled water, which takes on the delicious scent of the gum arabic.

Nettarine Fountain, Fès

Alcohol

The formal Muslim approach to alcohol is simple – it is forbidden on religious grounds. However, in practice, alcohol is available in Morocco, and drinking is permitted in certain areas, under certain conditions (in licensed hotels and bars) although traditional families do not serve it as a matter of course. Many Moroccan men will drink wine, beer and spirits on occasion, although it is rare to see Moroccan women imbibing.

Wine and beer are freely available following the French model – supermarkets and even some epiceries have quite well-stocked sections. Very rough wines can be bought very cheaply – for around 22 dirham – but you can get some cheerful reds for around 50 dirham, hardly expensive. In fact, the cost of a wine is usually a pretty good indicator of its taste. Alcohol is also offered in most of the big hotels and some of the restaurants (which are often attached to the hotels).

Because wine is not a traditional part of Moroccan culinary life, matching wine to meal is really a matter of individual taste. However, the general rules apply quite well here – white wines marry best with seafood and white meats; reds with richer red meat tagines and couscous. However, the Moroccan *rosés* and **gris** (light red) wines work well with the spicy flavours of Moroccan food.

Wine labels

This tolerant approach to alcohol has its roots in the era of the French protectorate at the start of the century, when many vineyards were planted in Morocco's rich soil. Vines flourished due to the sympathetic climate and conditions, particularly around Fès and Meknès, and south of Casablanca. However, the ambivalence of attitudes is evident in the fact that, while more than 60,000 hectares of land are presently under vines, much of the wine made in Morocco is very average (with notable exceptions) and many of the vineyards have been neglected or abandoned in the decades since the French left Morocco to the Moroccans.

Water seller, Meknès

Most grapes are sold on to the large Celliers de Meknès group, who take the raw pressed material and make it into pleasant, if mostly unremarkable, wines. This consortium, partly government owned, has been responsible for creating appellations in the French tradition, most importantly of the **Guerrouane** wine, which is one of the better Moroccan red styles. The Celliers de Meknès labels account for around 85% of the local market, and it exports over 1 million bottles to France, the Benelux countries (Belgium, The Netherlands and Luxembourg), the United Kingdom, Finland and the United States.

Moroccan white wines generally tend to be weaker than reds because the climate doesn't support white grapes particularly well. Most Moroccans seem to favour rosé or gris, which is a light, rather sweet, red that was developed in Morocco. Morocco could do much more with what it has in regard to vineyards and infrastructure, but it seems the Muslim government is reluctant to show too much enthusiasm for wine production, or to encourage joint ventures with other Mediterranean producers. As a result, the wine industry has fallen between the cracks somewhat, and been allowed to devalue – the general quality of wine has fallen. Perhaps the French were simply not in Morocco long enough to establish a culture of winemaking strong enough to coexist with an Islamic society.

In addition to winemaking, beer is also brewed in Morocco under the labels of Flag Speciale (Tangier) and Stork (Fès and Casablanca). The Flag label includes Flag Pilsener, Flag Speciale and Flag Export, a popular range of lagers (good for the climate here) sold in bottles and cans. Beer is available alongside wine in epiceries and supermarkets. Like wine, it is available in bars, hotels and some restaurants.

Reports in 1998 tell of Coca-Cola buying the Stork facility in Fès so beer may develop a higher profile in the future. The local beer is light, pleasant and easy to drink. Other light export beers like Budweiser are sometimes available, mainly in hotels.

home cooking & traditions

In the Moroccan home, food from the kitchen represents the state of the family. Delicious dishes are created with love, whereas disagreement will result in a sour spread. Only in the home is the real taste of Morocco found, along with the country's renowned hospitality. Here the kitchen is the heart, and food its communicator.

Moroccan cooking is defined not only by its flavours, but by a society. The traditional and enduring set-up in Morocco is staunchly patriarchal. Cooking takes its place as women's work, to be performed inside the home as a private art shared within the enclave of family and friends. It is only at the odd banquet or special event that cooks are expected to expose their skills to a wider audience. This essential marriage between women and cooking creates a number of characteristics in the Moroccan culinary culture.

Firstly, Moroccan food is a family-based cuisine, best experienced in private homes. Despite the existence of a handful of outstanding restaurants in Morocco, none of them can possibly outrate a good cook in her own kitchen. Moreover, in all the best restaurants, woman cooks are often the ones really directing proceedings – behind the scenes, of course.

This highlights another issue. In a country where many women still wear the veil and Islamic edicts on women are taken seriously, cooking may be the single most important means of expression for a woman. She may wear the veil, she may not even eat with her husband, she may have to prepare what she is told to prepare, but ultimately, she has the power to bring the food to the table.

For this reason, it is said in Morocco that cooking is a means of communication between husband and wife. A woman who is in a bad mood, disinterested or depressed will express her feeling through her cooking. She need not say a thing. A sensible husband will take note and take measures to repair the situation. Good cooking indicates marital and familial harmony in Morocco.

Similarly, when choosing a wife, all men in Morocco, no matter how young, know how to decipher a young woman's upbringing simply by tasting her food. A woman who is trying to impress a man or guests will cook the same sort of dishes as anyone else – the difference will be in preparation and presentation. Just as women are trained to cook, men are trained to taste, and any reasonably sensitive young male will be able to tell the difference between his mother's **tajine** and his wife's. He may prefer one to the other, and it's up to him to be discreet, but he will know the difference.

This is another essential fact of Moroccan cooking. It is ultimately dependent on the specific input of the cook. The same dish can be prepared in any number of ways. Each woman is proud of her own special additions, subtractions or variations. She may use more or less coriander. She may add ingredients at different times. If she is 'modern', she will use a lot less oil and butter, and may abhor the taste of **smen** (preserved butter). All of her special tricks, tastes and refinements will be more or less applauded by her husband and children, who will thus define her method to a great degree.

Shooting the breeze, Rabat

It's common for husbands either not to comment, or even slightly criticise, the cooking of their wives. This avoids the dangers of the evil eye, which may be attracted to him if he boasts about how fabulous she is. It also keeps his most precious asset on her toes. Too much criticism would be dangerous, however – a woman can communicate her resentment through bad cooking, or through dishes she knows her husband doesn't like. How is he to know what was available that day at the market?

Having stated this, we have been openly told by many more enlightened husbands about the marvellous cooking of their wives. Most of them proudly say that their wives cook in the 'modern' Moroccan manner. Certainly, these husbands think in the modern Moroccan manner which may become, by force of economy, prevalent, as more and more women are educated as professionals, join the workforce and no longer have time to cook in the time-honoured way.

Despite these isolated references to modern cooking (which mostly refer to a lighter style of food for the weight-conscious, another modernity), another major feature of Moroccan cooking is its adherence to tradition.

The culinary art is passed down from mother to daughter as part of her birthright. As cooking is so intimately connected with her sense of womanhood, a young woman will be eager to know all the culinary secrets her mother can impart. She will, in any event, have grown up in the kitchen assisting her mother with the daily preparation of meals. In a country where many women are still unable to read or write, the oral transmission of the craft, along with what is essentially a long and gradual apprenticeship, is crucial. There are very few standard cook books in Morocco because cooking is not something learnt from books. It is female and uneducated but wise and artful. There is a magical and transformative element to it. However, the most widely read book is *Moroccan Cuisine* by Latifa Bennani-Smires (see Recommended Reading before the Eat Your Words chapter).

Think of a Moroccan woman in all her facets. She can tie her hair up, tie her baby on to her and work the fields all day. But she will also possess robes for special occasions, when she may appear decked in all her finery, made-up and glamorous. Make this image a metaphor for Moroccan food. On one hand it is simple peasant food, on the other, it is elaborate and complex, showcased in banquets to mark festivals, weddings, death and birth.

While each woman prepares her food differently, the enduring themes of Moroccan food are the same the country over. Tradition is revered in Morocco, and experimentation is looked upon with distrust. Women, especially, are discouraged from striking out on their own, and definitely not in the area of cooking which equates with the family – improvisation is one thing, change is another. So recipes stay the same. Banquets stay the same. The cooking evolves, but as slowly as a good tajine cooks.

Shopping, Essaouira

One of the probable reasons why the slow-cooking method took hold in Morocco is because it gives women time to do everything they have to do. The tajine can be put on early in the morning, cook itself, and be ready at midday. In between, there are children to be looked after, fields to be tilled, water and firewood to be collected and many other tasks. One of the probable reasons why food in the cities is more elaborate than food in the country is that city women usually have more resources and more time.

The most fascinating thing to watch in a Moroccan kitchen is the hands of the woman cooking. Be it grand or humble, each kitchen is really only as good as the hands doing the cooking within it. It is as if these women, veiled, often uneducated and inarticulate in the outside world, have developed a sophisticated language of their own in their own kingdom, the kitchen.

The hands are absolutely critical in the preparation of couscous, for example. The steaming grains are winnowed twice through seasoned hands unbothered by the heat. This will determine whether the couscous is light and palatable, or stodgy and heavy. Heavy, damp couscous is an anathema to a good Moroccan cook (see Couscous in the Staples & Specialities chapter).

In measuring out herbs and spices, the hands know the quantities – a handful or a pinch can mean many different things. Hands know how to knead pastry and when the kneading should be done. Hands know how to pound the mortar and when the consistency is right. Hands grate vegetables and rub the garlic and salt paste into meat. Fingers prod meat, mix ingredients, tap pans, flick water.

The secret of Moroccan cooking lies in the hands. To learn how to cook Moroccan food, the student needs to watch and to touch in a harmonious coordination of hand and eye.

EATING EN FAMILLE

Casablanca is not a pretty town, and inhabitants of other Moroccan cities are dismissive of it. However, it has a modernity and vitality that is very attractive, and it's one of the best places in Morocco to see the combination of old and new. It was my first introduction to Morocco, and the food I tasted there –*chez* Nahmiah, her husband Abdelrahmin and their six daughters – was some of the best I tasted anywhere in the country.

The house was a modern, bald-faced terrace, unremarkable from the front, in a small street off the main road to Marrakesh. Inside, it opened out onto three levels. Communal living quarters were on the middle level, with the kitchen at the back, a small foyer with bathrooms on two sides, and the main living and eating room across the front.

Each room served a specific purpose. I was lodged in the magnificent main reception/dining room, and each night after the evening meal was cleared away, a bevy of dark-eyed daughters made up my bed with exquisite, hand-embroidered sheets (the gold thread was a bit scratchy, but I wasn't complaining as I lay there looking at the intricate ceiling).

As in most Moroccan households, the main meal, which Nahmiah spent the morning preparing, is at midday. A typical meal would be either an enormous tajine, or on Friday, a couscous.

She cut, washed, diced, grated, boiled and watched. She threw handfuls of this and pinches of that at the chicken tajine being prepared on a small gas burner in the corner. On the stove, she cooked vegetables for the salads; eggplant, tomato and onion laced with sweet Moroccan garlic; zucchini, cumin and black pepper; sweet green peppers and tomato with paprika and a splash of hot cayenne. She was also preparing a couscous for me to try (it wasn't Friday but I had, rather innocently, expressed a wish to try a real couscous and thus it was to be) and was making it at the same time on one of the cooktop burners.

As she grated carrot for the carrot salad (later she added lemon and orange flower water), Nahmiah told me how her mother had taught her the craft and lore of the kitchen. When she first got married, she said, she had been very nervous about her skills. Mothers-in-law are traditionally quite severe in Morocco and Nahmiah knew that she needed to be able to cook well in her new home, if she were to avoid being treated with contempt.

She related how she had been asked to prepare a fish tajine, regarded as very difficult for a novice. She passed with flying colours and her **belle-mere** (Mother-in-law) softened towards her. She laughed as she told me she was lucky that she was a good cook because, after six pregnancies, she had not yet provided a son and heir. She confided however that her husband didn't mind and was besotted with his tribe

Maison D'Hote, Fès

of girls. "**Inshallah**" (God wills it), she said resignedly, and laughed again. She checked the tajine quickly, removed the chicken livers and giblets, mashed them finely and returned the mixture to the tajine. This would thicken the sauce, she explained.

The salad vegetables were ready and removed from the cooker to cool. The couscous sauce was simmering away in the mijotte. Nahmiah checked to see what stage it was at, stirred gently with the pointed end of the spoon, and started to rub the chickpeas under water to remove the skins. When she was finished, she checked the couscous again, and started to prepare the grains.

Nahmiah's sister-in-law had actually made the couscous and given it to her for the occasion. I felt very honoured. Handmade couscous is becoming less and less common, as instant couscous (which, if well-handled, is very good) makes inroads.

She washed the grains first in the gas'a, then poured a portion into the kaskahs, leaving the lid off. About five minutes later she added the rest of the grains and let the whole lot steam for about 20 minutes. Then she removed the grains, poured them back into the gas'a, and added cold water, salt and a tiny dash of oil. She worked the grains with her hands, raking them backwards and forwards. Later, she would repeat the process, this time adding butter at the end.

I confess that I didn't believe that all this movement was necessary and thought she was being extravagant. I had made couscous before, according to the directions on the packet, and it said nothing of this. When I tasted Nahmiah's couscous, I knew why so much action was involved; it was vastly superior to my heavy stodge.

It was time to eat. Abdelrahmin had returned. The girls reappeared. Abdelrahmin graciously reminded me to wash my hands by gently showing me to the more glamorous of the two bathrooms.

An aunt was preparing tea in the reception room, which had been magically cleared of my extraordinary bed. The aunt – one of the zillion Fatimas who live in Morocco – was squatting in front of the **siniyya** (tea tray), and stuffing mint into the pot. She then put a large amount of crumbly sugar on top. After waiting for it to brew, she poured tea into a glass, inspected it, and poured it back into the pot. Then she poured in earnest and the tea was served by one of the smaller girls. While I drank my tea, I ate one of the biscuits being offered to me.

A table had appeared, covered in heavily embroidered cloth and a clear plastic sheet. It was placed in the corner of the room surrounded on two sides by **banquettes** (padded benches). Chairs were brought in from another room. We were seated, me as visitor in the plum position on one of the banquettes beside Abdelrahmin. A flurry of daughters appeared, bearing salads. All but two of the middle girls and Nahmiah were seated and eating. Bread was passed around the table by the eldest girl.

Nahmiah had kindly positioned little coffee spoons in each of the salads for my benefit; I tried anyway to pinch up salad with my bread held firmly in my right hand with moderate success.

After a while, the salads were pushed to the outer edge of the table. The daughters appeared again, bearing the tajine which was meltingly delicious. Olives were scattered down the side of the tajine – purplish, plump and sweet-tart. I had never tasted better olives and haven't since. Abdelrahmin elegantly sought out the most delectable bits of chicken and placed them in front of me on the tajine.

At one stage I forgot my manners and inadvertently licked my fingers. I looked up to see how the family would react but they politely ignored my transgression.

I was a slow and awkward eater but even so I was getting full, and the spectacular couscous was yet to come. The tajine was removed along with the small detritus of bones.

The couscous arrived with the two girls and Nahmiah, all of whom pulled up chairs and sat down. This slightly informal approach was probably due to so many women living under one roof, as well as Abdelrahmin's easy-going, gregarious nature. The fact that I was a foreign female journalist may also have had something to do with it. If it had been male friends or associates that Abdelrahmin was entertaining, all the women would have stayed well out of sight.

My appetite had disappeared with the tajine, but Nahmiah urged me to continue eating. Weakly I attempted to create a ball of couscous in my right hand but failed dismally. Halfway between plate and mouth the misshapen thing disintegrated. Abdelrahmin made one up for me, and Nahmiah fetched a large spoon. The couscous – replete with pumpkin, onions, raisins and chickpeas – was deliciously scented and the meat exquisitely tender even though I was extremely full.

I drank a little water and took a breather by undoing my belt. I had already been warned that drinking too much during a meal may be taken as an impolite gesture; it could signify that I didn't like the food and was filling my stomach with water instead. There was very little room left in mine anyway.

We finished the meal with fresh fruit and dates and then, of course, more mint tea, a refreshing contrast to the fragrant spices of the meal. At this point, the table was removed completely, and I was invited to relax on the banquettes as I sipped.

Sitting back, a smile slowly spread across my face. Only now did I fully understand what Moroccans mean when they refer to **shabaan** (complete satiation).

Utensils

Certain utensils are common to all households in Morocco, be they rich or poor, urban or rural.

Tajine Slawi

The tajine is made from earthenware, and should be cured before use. The pointed lid is glazed on the outside and unglazed on the interior. Tajines come in various sizes, from tiny to feed one or two, to a huge feeding up to 20. The plate of the tajine is quite shallow, with a grooved lip to take the lid snugly. It is important that the plate and top fit together well as tajine cooking is long and slow. Every sized tajine has an accompanying cooker which sits underneath filled with charcoal (see Tajines in the Staples & Specialities chapter).

Majmar

These are receptacles for charcoal and sit underneath the tajines, fitting into the base of the plate. They are available in various sizes, depending on the size of the tajine plate and are usually made of earthenware. Majmar made of iron or copper are used to support and heat the warqa pan (see Savoury Pastries in the Staples & Specialities chapter). Rectangular iron majmar are used as charcoal braziers for grilling brochettes and kebabs. These containers have small serrations on either side to hold the sticks (called m'ghazel, made of iron or silver) steady. This type of brazier can also be used to grill fish. In this case, a butterfly grill is used to hold the fish.

Tangine bases drying in the sun

KITCHENS IN MOROCCO

Styles of kitchen in Morocco, like kitchens all over the world, are subject to the affluence of the families who build them. The more money spent, the more sophisticated they become, especially in cities.

The nature of Moroccan cooking requires little of the gadgetry which litters the kitchens of many other countries. While some Moroccan women have gadgets such as blenders, many prefer to use the old ways – mortar and pestle, and slow heating – to achieve the result they want.

There is no gas network in Morocco so all gas cooking is done with portable bottles which can be bought from the **souq** (market). Every morning in Moroccan villages women ambling home on donkeys laden with gas bottles are a common sight. I have never seen anyone cooking with electricity in Morocco – most Moroccans dismiss it as an impossibility.

Urban Moroccans with a reasonable income prefer to have kitchen benchtops made of marble. Stainless steel sinks are also common. These materials are favoured because they are hard-wearing and hygienic – marble does not degenerate and is easy to sluice down.

By contrast, country kitchens can be very basic indeed. I visited the kitchen of a woman in a tiny High Atlas village, who prepared a simple but delicious tajine in what I discovered to be the most rudimentary of circumstances. Khadija's kitchen consisted of little more than a low, draughty room beneath the house, where the livestock was stabled also each night.

Along one side of this room there was a raised earth platform on which the fire was built to boil tea and create charcoal for the tajine **majmar** (see Majmar under Utensils opposite). The room was entirely blackened with the soot of many fires. It had no running water, no electricity and no refrigeration. There was a small gas bottle in the corner which Khadija confessed she used infrequently, and two blackened majmar, one large, one small. On the corner of the raised platform was an earthenware pot with two old wooden spoons sticking out of it. No other utensils were in evidence, although Khadija later told me that she kept two knives and a few basic bowls including a couscoussier upstairs, as the room was not secure. She kept any spare spices or couscous in jars and pots upstairs also. There were no windows and the only light and ventilation came in from the doorway. Khadija's cave-like kitchen was kept very tidy.

Despite her house-proud rigour I was distressed to hear that this woman, probably only in her early thirties, had lost two very young children to something that sounded like dysentery. She carried her third child, a ruddy faced, healthy-looking little girl, on her back like a possum, even while preparing the meals.

Many other kitchens in the bled (countryside) of Morocco are just as simple as Khadija's. Often, groups of houses will share an outdoor oven built out of earth. These large mound-like structures can be seen adjoining the mud houses like enormous beehives.

In the event of a feast, almost everyone in the village contributes something, or a **mashwi** (barbecued lamb) is prepared by the host family. Khadija explained that in the absence of refrigeration, preparation needs to be swift and communal.

Contrast Khadija's country kitchen with a typical kitchen belonging to a family that might be termed middle-class, living in the centre of Casablanca. Nahmiah had six children, all girls, all exquisite. Lined up to greet the foreign visitor, they reminded me of the Russian babushka dolls who all look the same, but diminish in size to fit inside each other. The eldest girls were doing very well at school and likely to go on to university, said Nahmiah, proudly. Nevertheless, the eldest girls helped her in the kitchen.

The kitchen was much smaller than I expected for such a large family house and quite spartan, though light and pleasant. Nahmiah cooked her tajines on a bunsen burner type arrangement in one corner of the room on the floor. Two large exposed gas bottles provided the gas for cooking.

Nahmiah had a stove with a cooktop, but preferred to use the burner for most of her cooking. She liked to sit on the floor to do this. She explained that she would cook side dishes such as salads on the cooktop, and only occasionally used the stove as one of the children took her bread to the community oven to be baked. Her benchtops were a pale-coloured marble and there was a double stainless steel sink for washing up. I reflected that one of the benefits of eating by hand was the fact that there was much less washing up to do each time. A decent-sized refrigerator stood in one corner. The kitchen was spotless.

Nahmiah possessed a range of tajines, and bowls for the making of bread and pastries. She had round majmar for the tajines, a rectangular one for the grilling of **brochettes** (kebabs) and two well worn but shiny couscoussiers. Her cooking utensils were simple – wooden spoons, a few knives and a few cutlery sets for gauche visitors.

She explained that when she holds a banquet, other women in the family come to help her. In this case, she would prepare most of the food. Nahmiah said that she always buys **warqa** pastry leaves from the local expert (it's so difficult to make oneself, you may as well leave it to the experts), with others helping in Nahmia's kitchen, or preparing their own specialities at home and bringing them on the day.

Other urban kitchens are very well-appointed and indistinguishable from any modern western version. Fatima's kitchen in Rabat was as

Detail of the brass door of Darel-Makhzen (Royal Palace), Fès el-Jdid, Fès

handsome as the rest of the house, with warm-toned marble bench-tops, plenty of (laminated) cupboard space, and a huge fridge with a generous freezer. Many Moroccan women have embraced the use of **congeles** (frozen food), although Fatima pointed out that it was now so fashionable to buy congeles, that many women had forgotten that it should really only be used for convenience. In her case, the freezer was dominated by two huge bags of diced, frozen herbs – coriander and parsley – which she used liberally in her dishes.

Fatima cooked on top of her four ring cooktop and said she rarely used the tajine these days except for presenting dishes. Instead, Fatima used the **mijotte** (pressure cooker) for her tajines and couscous. This western introduction has revolutionised the process of cooking for many Moroccan women. While most Moroccans, male and female, will enthusiastically attest to the particular deliciousness of a tajine cooked in earthenware on a traditional **majmar**, many women now cook with the mijotte as a matter of course. Often, the contents of a large pot – in Fatima's case, a large metal pot – are transferred late in the cooking process to the pressure cooker. The cooking time is significantly reduced while the flavour is not lost and the meats are cooked to a melting softness.

Typically, this family had a full set of Chinese-style plates and bowls. This type of crockery can be bought at most large Moroccan souqs in porcelain and in plastic. Most women prefer these to the native, heavier earthenware pottery, which are not designed to function as plates for individual servings.

Fatima set the table with a collection of these small plates, and put her salads into small bowls from the same set. Spices were kept in small jars with cork tops on the bench, or in glass jars in the cupboard.

Fatima favoured traditional implements to aid her cooking – in particular the large, wooden spoons with pointed handles used to lift whole chickens in and out of the pot. The family ate with their hands, so cutlery was sparse. Fatima kept some larger slotted spoons and ladles seemingly for display. A collection of knives, grater and colanders was kept near the sink. There was no microwave and no dishwasher.

Couscoussier

A two-part metal steamer – usually aluminium – used for making couscous. The upper part of the couscoussier is called the **kaskahs.** It is perforated with holes to allow steam to come through from the lower and larger part. Both parts have handles on either side and the kaskahs has a lid. The two parts should fit snugly together.

Tbik

A large, round wicker basket, closely woven, usually threaded with bright colours. Used for winnowing and separating couscous grains before cooking. Sometimes used as a plate for bread.

Tbaq/Tbicka

A large wicker basket in two parts used for storing bread. Looks rather like a tajine, with its large, pointed cover. The bottom part is a deep bowl shape. The pointed cover is garnished with a copper top.

Spoons and other utensils

Tobsil dial Warqa

This is a circular plate with a shallow lip, used upturned for making warqa, or right side up to make **bastila** pie (pigeon or other poultry in pastry). A tobsil is usually made of iron coated with copper.

Maqla dial trab

A large, round earthenware plate used to prepare both **rghayif** and **beghrir** pancakes.

Gas'a
A shallow wooden or earthenware plate with sloping sides, used to make pastry for breads and pastries.

Mahraz & Yad Lmahrahz
Mortar and pestle.

Quettara
Alembic used for distilling rose and orange flower water.

Gharbahl
A sieve made either with silk or fine iron filaments, used to separate grains and flour.

Tanzheer
A very large pot used to cook **khli'** (preserved meat). The largest can take up to 50kg.

Pots of various shapes and sizes, earthenware pots are used to store grain, khli' and smen, olives and other foodstuffs. Wooden spoons, with circular bowls and pointed ends, are used to eat **hrira** and other soups, as well as stirring and prodding food.

celebrating
with food

Being Moroccan, Muslim and Mediterranean, people here have much to celebrate. Islamic tradition, rites of passage, even funerals, all mark times of gratitude and recognition. And with each celebration comes a culinary spread that includes specialities and delicacies seen at no other time – foods that bind both family and nation.

The sacred is present in practically all Moroccan cooking, from the "**Bismillah**" (in the name of God) that a woman says in the kitchen as she begins preparations, to the "**al-hamdou li-Allah**" (thanks be to God) that guests say at the end of the meal, everything is paced by short prayers and subtle rituals. From the choice of ingredients used for religious or family feasts, right to the final cooking, the tradition of the Prophet is respected and applied.

The first step is the choice of products used: Islam prohibits meat deriving from animals whose throats have not been cut according to correct ritual, meat such as pork, considered noxious to human health, and alcoholic beverages. All other products are allowed. Certain foods such as milk and dates are favoured as symbols of hospitality and welcome. These foods were certainly those with which the Prophet was most familiar, given that he was born and lived in Arabia, the cradle of Islam.

In Morocco, as in all Muslim countries, the year is dotted with religious festivals. The symbolic foods which accompany each occasion are integral parts of the celebrations. There are six main religious festivals: **Ramadan** (the month of fasting); **Aid Seghir** (the end of Ramadan); **Aid el Kebhir** (the feast of the lamb); **Hegira** (the period of the new year); **Moharam** (the first day of the new year); **Achoura** (the 10th Day); and finally **Mouloud** (the celebration of the Prophet's birthday). All these feasts and ceremonies gradually change seasons, since they are based on the lunar months which shift by 13 days every year. Dates of the ceremonies are jealously kept. Family festivities fit around these dates.

Ramadan is a holy month divided up into prayers, fasting and eating. According to the tradition of Islam, a month's fasting was adopted to give people time for reflection and introspection, to appreciate the value of food, to thank God for it and to understand the hunger that wracks the poor. But Ramadan is also a time when cooks excel themselves. Competing for inventiveness – and piety – households concoct invigorating and restorative dishes rich in sugar, fat and flour. Three meals are served each evening; **ftur, acha** and **shour**.

Ftur breaks the fast and is often composed of the soup, **hrira**, served with dates (recommended by the Prophet for breaking the fast), fresh milk and **griwash** (honey cakes) sprinkled with sesame seeds. Each ingredient is loaded with symbolism and sacred meaning and has a direct connection with religion.

Acha, which gets its name from the final prayer of the day, is a late meal. Some people take it directly after ftur, others take it several hours later in the course of the evening. Composed of meats, breads, vegetables and fruits, it is a heavy meal.

RAMADAN

It was Ramadan and it was cold. The streets were crowded with people anxiously waiting for the evening call to prayer, so they could break their fast. At the first sounds of "Allah akbar" from the neighbourhood mosque, children immediately scrambled home, labourers came in from the fields and the women prepared the repast. The first course was hrira, a delicious hardy soup, and khubz ('chubs' of bread) accompanied by olive oil, jam and butter. Everyone got a hard-boiled egg, which holds great symbolism in Moroccan culture. Families celebrating births frequently gave me hard-boiled eggs, which are believed to symbolise fertility.

The sounds of the latest Latin telenova translated into classical Arabic could be heard from the television – and every Moroccan family in Jorf, Er-Rachidia (the village where I was living) had a television. The main character of this show had the entire village glued to her fate. It was so cold I could see my breath indoors, but the hardy soup and tea warmed me up. As everyone slurped their hrira, the women were already busy preparing for the next meal, lamb tajine, for 10pm.

The best meal during Ramadan was 'dinner', not because of the food per se, but because of the familial feeling that went along with it. At around 4.30am a man came through the streets banging a loud drum to wake everyone and remind them that they had to eat before dawn. Rising sleepily from my bed, more tired than hungry, I was handed warmed-up bread and yet another lamb tajine. Wrapped in blankets, we waited for the mint tea to warm us up. We ate in silence and returned to sleep, preparing to wake to yet another day of fast.

April Cohen

Shour, from the word **sahar** (to keep watch) is the last meal before dawn and the beginning of the fast. Often composed of substantial foods that 'stick to your ribs', it is designed to help make the day of fasting more bearable. **Rghayifs** (crepes stuffed with meat), **beghrir** (honeycombed crepes spread with butter and honey) and **malwi** (pancakes spread with butter and honey) go to make up the bulk of the meal, which is often finished with a dry couscous sprinkled with sugar and cinnamon and accompanied by fresh or curdled milk.

Ramadan dishes are all rich in sugar, grains and milk, which are the three basic foundations of an ancestral culinary culture stemming from environment, history and religion.

The month of Ramadan ends in the festival Aid Seghir. A small climax compared to Aid el Kebhir, it's celebrated the day after the last day of

Ramadan. In the course of this festival, the house is sprinkled with milk as a sign of friendship. The head of the household buys **fetra** (a mixture of equal parts of the grains wheat, barley and corn) which is then distributed to the poor.

Two main dishes are prepared on this occasion. In the morning a soup, based on fine semolina flavoured with aniseed and accompanied by griwash, is served. This soup was dear to the Prophet which explains why the tradition survives, because the soup is neither rich nor particularly tasty. Once upon a time, the fast would have been broken by everyone with a simple spoonful of honey.

After the midday prayer, a delicately contrasting dish of chicken and pickled pumpkin is prepared. This sweet and sour dish is highly prized in Fès. In other parts of the country the dish takes another form, being stuffed with semolina and almonds and flavoured with cinnamon.

The feast of the sacrifice of Aid el Kebhir stems from the sacrifice made by the prophet Ibrahim (Abraham). In the Koran, Abraham was willing to sacrifice his son, but was prevented from doing so by God, who suggested a sheep instead. Muslims have accordingly returned to the sacrifice of the sheep during the feast of Aid el Kebhir which coincides with the end of the prophet's pilgrimage to Mecca.

During the weeks before the holiday, sheep are bought and carried home to be fattened for the feast. They can be kept in kitchens, on rooftops, or in small garden plots before being slaughtered, mid morning on the day of Aid el Kebhir. This task is performed by the head of the household or sometimes a neighbourhood butcher. Every family, rich or poor, endeavours to have at least one sheep for this occasion. The quality of the beast may depend on the affluence of the family, but not to have a sheep is a sign of piteous poverty.

And so every family sacrifices a sheep, the feast providing an occasion to make rich and varied dishes. **Bulfahf** (grilled liver) and dewwahra (tripe spiced with a coriander and garlic sauce) are usually served for lunch – the smells released by the kebabs pervading every home. Strong green tea to aid digestion.

Aid el Kebhir lasts for as long as the fresh meat does, which depends on the means of each family. If several sheep are sacrificed in a wealthy home, part of the meat will be preserved in the form of **khli'**, which can keep for a whole year (see Meats in the Staples & Specialities chapter).

The main meals on the days following are all based on meat which is either steamed or served very hot and sprinkled with salt and cumin; or browned in a pan with **mhammar** (a sweet paprika sauce) or made into a mruziyya tajine.

Berber shepherd and his flock, High Atlas

Every part of the lamb is used allowing cooks to cover the spectrum of Moroccan meat dishes. **Hergma** is made from the lamb's trotters, with chickpeas and cracked wheat. This is often served at street stalls in large, bent enamelled plates. The lamb's brains are washed, cooked and combined with herbs and spices in a salad.

On **moharam** (the first day of the new year), a large couscous, symbol of abundance, is prepared with whatever vegetables are in season. Ten days later, on **achoura** (the 10th day), part of the khli' of Aid el Kebhir is used to make either a couscous or a tajine. This savoury dish symbolises the bridge between the feast of the sacrifice and the beginning of the new year, the Hegira.

SILENCE OF THE LAMBS (AND THE VEGETARIANS)

Walking the streets of Rabat, we paid little heed to the small flocks of tethered sheep at various points of the city. We raised our eyebrows when the urban sheep population threatened to take over, but it was only when we were awoken by the determined bleating of a flock of sheep on the roof of our hostel that we realised something special was afoot.

We had landed in Aid el Kebhir (the feast of the lamb). Celebrated to commemorate the sacrifice of a lamb which Allah exchanged for a son of Abraham, every family sacrifices a lamb around dawn on the day of the festival. The country muttons down the hatches for five days, during which lamb parts are consumed in astronomical qualities. My vegetarian companion was thrilled with our serendipity.

The days prior to the festival were frantic. In a spectacle not unlike the mayhem of last minute Christmas shopping, families tore around town trying to find the last available sheep or lamb. An elegant Moroccan on a small scooter balanced one on his shoulders as he weaved in and out of the city traffic. We saw a family driving home with their sacrificial lamb; parents in the front seat, young child in one back seat and the young Dolly in the other. She sat with her seat belt securely fastened and her little legs dangling over the edge of the seat. She seemed quite content, oblivious to her fate. Surely, we thought, she was beginning to realise that something was definitely amiss.

Waking before sunrise on the morning of the festival (by this time in Meknès), we were greeted by the now omnipresent bleating drifting over the rooftops of the medina. As the sun rose, the bleating gradually faded, as family after family slaughtered their recently acquired lamb. Knowledge of the ovine genocide was eerie. Soon, family parties and celebrations spilled out into the streets and the macabre mood was

A few months later, the festival of **mouloud** marks the celebration of the birth of the prophet, Mohammed. **Assida** (a thick, cooked cereal with a durum wheat semolina base, moistened with butter and honey) is served, accompanied by dates or honey cakes. This poor man's dish symbolises humility before God. For the midday meal, culinary traditions do not rely on any one dish, but every family endeavours to serve something based on red or white meat.

Moroccans, firstly as Muslims and secondly as Mediterraneans, love to celebrate the different stages of life. Births and baptisms, weddings and funerals are a time for expressing joy or sadness, and cooking seems like the ideal companion for such ceremonies. Containing diverse traditions

replaced by a carnival atmosphere. We felt quite isolated without a party to attend and my companion – under no circumstances – would gatecrash. It was a few hours later, when we ventured outside for food, that we made our most significant discovery; for the next four days, no restaurants or snack bars would open.

Presented with such circumstances, it is amazing what humans will do for sustenance. No, we didn't eat the passengers from the fuselage. Luckily, bread, a staple of the Moroccan diet, continued to be baked and was available from the tobacco kiosks dotted all around town. Combined with the ubiquitous spreadable cheese and jams, we survived the five days.

Meanwhile, as we barely survived, a vegetarian's nightmare materialised on the streets of Meknès. Nothing went to waste as every part of the lamb was consumed in a variety of ways. As we smelled the roasted, chargrilled or boiled lamb being prepared throughout the medina, we wondered how the locals were coping with their similarly monotonous diet, and if lamb was, perhaps, beginning to lose its appeal.

Finally, the festival ended and the restaurants opened again. Licking our lips, we rushed to gorge on all we had missed during the festival – tangy tajines, creamy couscous and, eh, various vegetables (we were feeling light-headed but we still loved alliteration). Our jaws dropped, mid-drool, when we realised that lamb was the only offering. Amazingly, even after the gluttony of the preceding days, there was still some of the damn stuff left. Even more surprising, there was still a demand for it. After much negotiation with a bemused waiter – he couldn't understand why we didn't want lamb – we settled for the only fresh food he could rustle up; two plates full of fried eggs, the most enjoyable meal we've ever had.

Geoff Stringer

and acting as a melting pot for all the cultures that have succeeded each other in Morocco, the cuisine used in Moroccan family ceremonies today reproduce habits, dishes and traditions in which paganism vies with Islam. Modernity, more or less assimilated, mixes with ancient rites.

Baptism clearly demonstrates this. In Morocco, births always give rise to great rejoicing. The day the baby is born, soft-boiled eggs and cakes are handed around to the children of the house so they can 'adopt' the new baby. For her first breakfast, the new mother will eat a hen if the baby is a boy, or a rooster if the baby is a girl, a practice that symbolises the marriage of the child. In any event, the mother will feed herself mainly with meat broth.

On the seventh day after the birth, the tables groan with dishes that vary according to the region and the town. Many include hrira with chicken, served with oval-shaped anise and sesame seed **faqqa** biscuits, nuts and dates; liver of a sheep (the liver being a symbol of love, everyone must taste it to love the child); rghayifs, beghrir and mlawi; and sweet couscous. The last is recommended for the mother to regain her strength and improve her milk.

In keeping with the prescriptions of the **sunna** (the tradition established by the Prophet), a sheep is sacrificed and the child's name is officially announced. The sheep – several of them if the family is rich – will be eaten at the midday meal, cooked in a sauce and never barbecued.

Marriage is placed under divine protection and must appear under the most favourable auspices. All the most auspicious signs are accordingly enlisted along with all the symbolic traditions and prayers. Bouquets of mint and marjoram, rose and orange flower waters are used – symbols of purity, sweetness, prosperity and happiness. The symbol of prosperity is also found in the loaf of bread the mother-in-law slips under the arm of her daughter-in-law as soon as she arrives.

Already a week before the wedding, the mother will offer the future bride dishes that 'no ladle has stirred' so that her marriage will be peaceful and untroubled.

Wedding festivals traditionally lasted a week with numerous receptions. Today, they usually last a day, often with a feast in the afternoon, a dinner and an evening party that often goes until dawn.

The couple's first day together begins with the breakfast ceremony, with the mother of the bride sending breakfast trays to the young newlyweds and their guests. The menu consists of **sfenzh** (donuts), milk, rice pudding and sheep's heads.

Feast day menus are often composed of refined and expensive dishes such as **bastila** (pidgeon or poultry pie), **mashwi** (chicken with preserved

Guardians at the entrance to the Moulay Ismail Mausoleum, Meknès

lemons and olives), and **tfaya** (mutton with almonds and hard-boiled eggs). These dishes are served on large, ornate plates, placed in the middle of low tables. The guests serve themselves either directly from the plate or from side plates reserved for the purpose.

Before and after the wedding, the bride visits the **hammam** (bath house) to purify herself. On her return, her parents send her trays of food with mint tea: coffee, flavoured with orange flower water and cinnamon; **krachels** (small, sweet bread rolls flavoured with aniseed and a sprinkling of sesame seeds); soft boiled eggs; and roasted almonds. These foods are supposed to help the bride regain her strength after the vigour and excitement of the wedding ceremony and, hopefully, her first night of marriage.

Funerals are also an occasion for special cooking as fires are not lit for three days in the houses of the family, relatives, and friends close to the recently deceased.

The first full meal comprises bread, honey and fresh butter. These noble products and their natural quality represent the acceptance by all of the accomplishment of divine will. Tea is prohibited because of its association with joy, and black coffee is served in glasses in the kitchen to avoid all semblance of ceremony.

A simple, dry couscous is brought over by neighbours and is served on **miadi** (simple, rimmed round tables) along with jugs of fresh milk. Similar meals are served on the second day.

On the third day after the death, the first meal prepared by the family is known as the 'dinner of the tomb', and it excludes festive dishes. Couscous with vegetables – and sometimes, in towns and cities, with meat, turnips and chickpeas, or onions and raisins – is the norm.

On the first Friday following this dinner the ceremony known as **tafriq** (from the word for sharing) takes place. Bread and figs are handed out at the cemetery. From this day on, life resumes its rights in the house of the deceased. Butter and honey are always on offer but are served at the end of the meal. Visitors who continue to come to offer their condolences are served roasted almonds, hard-boiled eggs and krachels. On the 40th day after the death, enormous quantities of couscous are made at home and taken, as charity to the poor, to the town's mosques.

regional
variations

Encompassing deserts, mountains and coastline, Morocco covers the full geographical gamut. Consequently, dishes often change according to climate and local produce. Although major themes in Moroccan cuisine remain remarkably cohesive, tendencies such as the use of pepper or seafood, rather than strict differences, mark the culinary differences between regions.

There are dishes definitely associated with specific cities or regions, but on the whole, Moroccans are quite liberal when exchanging and adapting within broad themes.

The cooking of Fès is said to be among the finest in Morocco. Regarded as the home of the great classic Moroccan dishes, Fès cooks traditionally use less sugar, adhere more strictly to tradition, and are very meticulous in preparation. Because of the wealth of the surrounding district, the ingredients are also traditionally of the highest quality. Most Fassi women have a slightly superior or aristocratic attitude, regarding other regional variations as rustic or unrefined at worst, colourful at best. This may or may not be the case in reality, but this is the tradition that holds sway even today. It is said that the finest **warqa** (pastry) makers come from

Sellu

Ingredients

- 1kg plain flour
- ½ teaspoon of aniseed seeds
- 500g almonds
- 500g castor sugar
- 1 teaspoon cinnamon
- 250g butter (melted)
- 1 pinch gum arabic (optional)
- 2 teaspoons of honey
- 250ml light oil, such as canola
- crystallised sugar (coffee sugar)
- 500g wholemeal flour
- 500g sesame seeds

Spread the sifted plain flour on a platter in a warm oven and cook until golden. Stir a few times during this process. At the same time, grill the sesame seeds lightly in a pan and put them through the blender – don't make the mixture too fine. Fry the almonds in the oil until golden; put a handful of these aside and pass the rest through the blender. Again, don't blend the mixture too finely.

Mix the cooked flour, sesame seeds, almonds, sugar, cinnamon, gum arabic and aniseed.

Into the oil left over from frying the almonds, fry the wholemeal flour. When it is golden, take the pan off the flame and add to it the honey and melted butter.

Mix the two mixtures together and shape it into a cone on a platter. Sprinkle the crystallised sugar over the cone. Decorate the cone with the leftover almonds.

Fès. Similarly, the couscous of Fès is more opulent. Also, it is from here that the extraordinary **sellu** derives – this is a rich dessert made especially for weddings with flour, toasted sesame seeds, fried almonds, **smen** (preserved butter) and honey.

The dishes of Marrakesh, a city bordering on the desert, tend to contain more pepper, while Rabat citizens favour unctuous sweetness and dried fruits. The north tends to bear a more Spanish influence, such as the existence of tapas bars in Tangier. While in the south, Berber influences abound with simpler dishes based on seasonal produce. For example, the region east of the Atlas mountains near Erfoud is famed for dates, which are added liberally to tajines and couscous. The middle Atlas is famed for its **mechoui** (barbecued lamb), although this dish has been adopted by all regions in Morocco. Berber bread is often unleavened, and cooked on hot flat stones

Two heads, Fès

It is in the southern sub-Sahara that such exotic meats as camel, gazelle and hedgehog are eaten. Like in Marrakesh, dishes here often contain more spice. This is due to the influence of Senegalese cooking, which is hotter and spicier than classic Moroccan. Many of the tribes in this region are of mixed race descent.

Coastal regions differ from the mountainous areas in the type of produce available – more fish, less dates, almonds and lamb is the most succinct way of describing this divide. For example, poultry and fish stuffed with almond paste – a very sweet, rich dish – is associated with the town of Safi on the coast, while the use of rice and vegetables is associated with the north.

Mountain and desert Berber dishes tend to be much simpler and more rustic. Where a Fès tajine will be a symphony of flavours and spices, a Berber tajine will incorporate perhaps only three ingredients and a couple of spices, depending on what the cook has on hand. A major factor influencing mountain Berber food is that women work in the fields all day, and thus have less time to cook. Furthermore, rural families are often not as wealthy. Despite this, meals are as tasty as their urban counterparts, often containing the freshest garden produce. The exception to this simplicity occurs at festivals or family celebrations, when food is showcased as part of the occasion and includes a wide array of tajines, couscous and salads.

Seafood

The best place to eat fresh fish is on the coast, and a multitude of tajines are prepared with local varieties of fish, including **tassargal** (a type of blue fish) caught off the coast in summer. Other types include sardines, turbot, sea bream, sole, mackerel, swordfish, tuna, as well as crustaceans such as crabs, shrimps, lobsters and clams.

Fish tajines require fish to be placed on a bed of bamboo and carrot or celery sticks, to prevent the skin sticking to the pot. Most fish is cooked with a marinade called **sharmoola** (see Sauces in the Staples & Specialities chapter). The Atlantic ports of Safi, Essaouira and, to a lesser extent, Casablanca and Tangier, are excellent places to try fresh local fish.

Stuffed fish is another notable speciality. In the gastronomic capital of Fès, it is made with the **alose** (shad) from the local River Sebou. In this rich, complex dish fish are stuffed with dates, themselves stuffed with chopped almonds and spices such as cinnamon and ginger. Shad with wild artichokes and shad with broad beans are also Fassi specialities.

In Rabat, where recipes are known for their sweetness, shad is prepared with cinnamon and raisins. Rabatti recipes typically include honey or prunes, often caramelised in a delicious reduction sauce.

Tetouan, along with other parts of the Rif Mountain area, is renowned for its stuffed fish dishes. These often incorporate rice, preserved lemons, onions and eggs. A rich, sweetened 'jam' made from tomatoes is sometimes used as a stuffing. This is found all over Morocco as an accompaniment to salad

A FINE KETTLE OF FISH

One of the most delicious meals to be had in all of Morocco is under a striped umbrella along the sea wall at Essaouira, where gulls wheel and screech as the fishermen bring in their catch. The fish are laid out on concrete slabs, doused frequently with salt water, and auctioned off. Little open-air cafes set up alongside the fish market offer the best fish of the day, spread out for you to select. Your choice is swiftly scaled, gutted, butterflied and grilled over a small charcoal fire. The fish is sometimes dusted with flour before cooking, and often a bowl of **sharmoola** (marinade) accompanies the meal. It is usually served with a simple salad of tomato, lettuce, olive oil and coarse rock salt, and a bowl of sliced **baguette** (long bread roll) often so fresh it's still warm. This is a sublimely simple but memorable meal that should not be missed. These cafe clusters can be found up and down the coast of Morocco, and offer the best and freshest fish.

dishes. This 'jam' is known as **matecha m'assala**, or by its French name, **confit de tomates**.

In Essaouira, the strength and cohesion of the Jewish community is evident and you're likely to come across specialities such as fish balls. **Breewaht** (triangular pastry) stuffed with fish is another Jewish favourite. Essaouian fish tajines are said to be the finest on the coast. Another Jewish dish, traditionally made on Friday for the Sabbath is **dafina**, best cooked for nearly 24 hours. It is customary to take this dish to the local baker's oven to cook slowly in the embers. Made with a variety of meats – cuts of beef, tongue, cow's feet – dafina can be made with chickpeas, rice or wheat.

Seafood platter

Meat

The most celebrated regional meat dishes in Morocco are Berber in origin. The famous mashwi, **khli'** (preserved meat), and the semi-preserved **mruziyya** (sweet & sour tajine) are typical Berber dishes which are found all over Morocco but are especially good in the traditional Berber communities of the Middle Atlas. Mashwi is particularly good here, where the proper pit can be dug to take an entire beast.

While evidence suggests that the Turks introduced skewered meats to the Moroccans, the Berbers insist that mashwi predates Turkish influence. Certain differences can be found in mashwi preparation. The most familiar and traditional way is to rub cumin and salt into the meat and barbecue the beast over an open fire. However, some sub-Saharan communities bake the lamb in large communal furnaces, and use the cumin and salt mixture only as condiments with which to eat the meat.

Meat tajines are found all over Morocco, and express their most fragrant combinations in cities such as Fès. In Marrakesh, a version of the tajine, the **tanzhiyya**, is often found. The principle of long, slow cooking is the same. The use of vegetables and spices depends on the cook rather than the region, although a preponderance of vegetables in certain areas, as well as seasonal variation, will determine the specific ingredients and their treatment. A typical tanzhiyya will include a cut of lamb or beef such as

DJEMMA EL-FNA

Whatever night of the week, Marrakesh's vibrant Djemaa el-Fna square is crowded. Resembling a year-round festival, it's a good place to try festive foods out of season and occasion. Against the din of hypnotic Gnaou music, Berber songs, and hippy Nass El-Ghiwane ballads, you will hear the voices of poets, comedians, fortune-tellers and impotence-curing herbalists. Not to be missed are the stalls dispensing sweet reddish-brown cinnamon tea from shiny bronze urns, along with plates of body-warming **tkaout**, the spicy but sweet chocolate-brown dessert, which is considered a tonic, and often served after births or during Ramadan.

There's everyday food at the Djemaa too but you can be sure there won't be a tourist in sight near the stalls selling sheep heads. The hair is singed off in a fire, then the head is cleaned in hot water and stewed with chickpeas. One whole head costs a princely Dr60 but usually you'll be given a carved-up portion of your favourite bits – everything but the eyes is eaten.

Margo Daly

DON'T MISS

Fes
- snacking on chickpeas while exploring the souq
- a walk around the Hôtel Palais Jamaï
- the finest couscous, bastila and tajines in the land

Meknès
- the tastiest olives
- the province of Khemisset, rich in wheat, olives and vines

Marrakesh
- tanzhiyya, a slow-cooked speciality
- a stroll in La Mamounia, host hotel to celebrities and royalty
- amelou, a paste made with honey and argan oil spread on bread
- spicy tajines made with camel meat

Rabat
- a pizza fix
- Café Maure, one of the best spots to enjoy a pot of mint tea

Essaouira
- a fresh fish meal at the harbour
- the fish markets

Casablanca
- the colourful central souq
- the fish restaurants along 'Ain Diab

The Atlas Mountains
- the best mechoui in the land
- dates and almonds of the Tafilelt region

The North
- tapas in Spanish-influenced Tangier
- briks, a savoury pastry native to Algeria
- a chicken tajine in the historic town of Tetouan

shoulder of lamb or an oxtail, spices such as garlic, cumin, ginger, paprika or cayenne, onions, coriander, parsley and perhaps preserved lemon and smen. Vegetables such as pumpkin, carrots, turnips or potatoes are sometimes added.

Poultry

K'dras, the delicious, oniony, saffron-hued chicken tajines cooked with lots of smen are examples of how regional differences operate in Morocco. In Fès, they are made without ginger, while in other cities and in the north, ginger is included. Similarly, some of the ginger-using areas also brown the chicken before cooking it in the tajine, while classic Fès cooks sniff at this idea. These slight differences are the only distinguishing regional feature.

Similarly, the individualistic people of the Rif Mountains rub chicken with cumin, a technique usually only associated with Berber-style lamb. In Marrakesh, chicken is roasted in the style *a la* mashwi. Many are speared whole on a spit and turned over an open fire, but without cumin.

Emshmel (chicken with lemon and olives) is most delicious in Khemisset, the rich hinterland between Fès and Meknès where the olives are finest.

Couscous

Couscous can be used in the simplest or the most complex of dishes, ranging from a fresh bean stew poured over the grains in the simple and delicious manner of mountain folk, to the riot of meat, vegetables and spices found in the high tradition of Fès. The sweetness associated with Rabat is expressed in the addition of honey to couscous dishes. Berber villagers sometimes use barley instead of semolina, or use green barley shoots with the grains. In Essaouira, maize meal is often used with a fish couscous, along with vegetables such as fennel and turnips. Tomatoes are used far more frequently on the coast with fish couscous and tajines than inland. Gourds grow easily in the southern parts of Morocco, and pumpkin couscous is associated with the area around Marrakesh.

shopping
& markets

Among the main attractions of Morocco are the **souqs** (markets). Ranging in size from the massive souq of Fès – which blossoms daily along the labyrinthine streets of the **medina** (old quarter) – to the smaller souqs typical of rural Morocco, they provide the opportunity to explore everything that this rich, resourceful land has to offer. And we're not just talking food.

The Arabs are masters at the art of buying and selling, and possess a strong tradition of canny commercial opportunism. This can be slightly intimidating, especially if you're used to buying from shops where prices of goods are non-negotiable. Nothing of this surety exists in the souqs, where everything is for sale, and the price is always adjustable. Learning how to bargain and how to play the game of shopping is the key to enjoying the marvellous diversity of a Moroccan souq, as well as coming away with some of the best goods at the best prices.

Everyone is expected to haggle as bargaining is one of the most strongly developed arts of Moroccan culture. There is an etiquette to it that can involve a great deal of rhetoric and flowery language, as well as mint tea, swapping of stories (often a diversionary tactic) and the cut and thrust of debate that can reach the heights of diplomatic skill.

Buying food can be less stressful or less exhilarating, depending on how you look at it. While bargaining is expected, vendors often have a set price per kg for goods, displayed on a piece of cardboard in front of the shop or trolley. If vendors – usually those selling from makeshift trolleys or a few crates on the ground – don't display the price, assume that they will sell for less than their opening quote.

The saying, 'they can see you coming' has special resonance in some of the souqs in major cities. Foreigners are obvious prey for vendors, especially in Marrakesh, where the sheer volume of tourists moving through the souqs (often in tour groups) has reduced the value of the experience while raising the price of goods. Even if you're an intrepid individual traveller, you'll inevitably be lumped in with the tour group crowd as vendors make no distinction. In Fès, Rabat, Meknès or Casablanca, the foreigner factor is often much less galling.

If you want to enter the fray of the souqs, and enjoy the experience, it's important to accept two things: learn to bargain with a good grace, and accept the fact that you will pay a bit more than the locals. It's all part of the ride.

DATE AT THE SOUQ

When at a souq you'll see dates displayed in amber-coloured piles and you can haggle for hours over the relative values of hard dried, soft dried or fresh. Vendors will try to entice you to their stalls by handing you huge, juicy dates stuffed roughly with a walnut or almond. You should always be able to taste before you buy – you may even be offered a cup of mint tea to complete the snack.

Returning home with the shopping, Chefchaouen

At the Souq

You may have heard about the colour, movement, smell and street theatre. Well, the typical Moroccan souq has it all. Donkeys awkwardly make their way through alleys of beckoning merchants and streams of shoppers. The mouth-watering smell of grilled meats mingles with the sharp tang of citrus fruit being squeezed, or the softer scent of rose petals displayed in great shallow wicker baskets. Peddlers shout songs about their wares. Vendors shout about what's available or bargain loudly with gesticulating shoppers. Visitors, pausing to gaze at great piles of dates, figs and almonds, are pursued and romanced by the vendor who presents an enormous date stuffed with a giant almond to seduce the taste buds (and hopefully a sale).

PICKPOCKETS

When travelling, there is always some risk of being harassed or having your belongings stolen. However, if you're careful and sensitive to local customs, then pickpockets or harassment in Morocco are no more likely than anywhere else.

Pickpockets exist everywhere, including Morocco. However the punishment for pickpocketing here can be severe and instantaneous, as we witnessed one afternoon in Rabat. While drinking coffee with Moroccan friends near the souq, we watched as a beggar approached each table asking for money. He was firmly turned away each time. Suddenly, a fracas erupted. It transpired that he had picked the pocket of an off-duty policeman who was relaxing there with a couple of friends. They stopped the beggar, and a torrent of harsh Arabic was exchanged. Then he was literally pulled by the scruff of his neck around to the back of the building where the policeman and his friends gave him a sound beating. Sound was the operative word. His shrieks pierced the atmosphere of the afternoon but nobody else seemed to even take notice.

The beggar – a young man who looked quite well dressed – survived. He had a bloodied lip and a bruised eye. As he limped off, the policemen and his friends returned to the table with the stolen wallet and continued drinking their coffee while the beggar stopped by the side of the road and pulled out a cigarette. He hailed a cab, jumped in, and the incident was finished. Rough justice, perhaps, but an indication of how unacceptable his behaviour was in the eyes of locals.

If your pockets are picked – and presumably you'll have taken all the steps to prevent this happening – then run for the nearest policeman and report it.

The head of a camel is displayed along with some of his other attributes – haunches, fillets and neck – next to a crate of cheeping, lively yellow chicks. Pastel-coloured nougat studded with almonds is stacked carefully in slabs like coloured terrazzo. At the foot of this gaudy tower sits a very old man selling four fat sausages of what looks like plastic-packaged English devon (complete with Arabic script on the packaging), two plastic squirter bottles of tomato sauce and single cigarettes from a packet of Marlboro. The souqs showcase all the life there is in Morocco and a trip to any one of them is a visit to Moroccan culture in its most vital form.

Souqs are as different as they are similar. It's this connection between diversity and similarity that makes them so fascinating. The old medinas of each town usually house the traditional souqs, where each vendor has a shop selling his own particular wares, ranged along the side of the street. You'll often see the craftsmen working wood, fabric, or cane basketry, while his goods are displayed in front.

In the major cities, each new part of town usually boasts a **marche centrale** (central souq). A legacy of the benevolent General Lyautey, who governed Morocco after its colonisation by the French, the new towns were built (and continue to expand) next to the medinas. Thus, the authenticity of the traditional Moroccan way of life now lives quite comfortably side by side with the more modern French endowment.

Where the division of the different types of produce in the souqs depends on a traditional location, or simply on space, the marches centrales sell food, food and more food in neatly divided sections. That is not to say that they are colourless – they are often the best places to buy good, fresh edibles and usually offer magnificent displays and lots of bustle and movement. Bargaining is generally less ferocious in the marches centrales, although it is still expected.

If you're looking for quality fresh food, go to the marche centrale. For colour and authenticity, go to the souq. Having said this, there are many, many food vendors in the souqs who sell excellent, fresh, wholesome food but it's sometimes more difficult to distinguish.

Given that most accommodation is usually near the newer section of town, the marche centrale may be the most convenient stop for provisions. In small towns, you may not have the luxury of a marche centrale, the only place to go may be the weekly food souq.

Generally speaking, hygiene is always slightly problematic in Morocco. The lack of refrigeration and the custom of hanging food out on display are two reasons, the water in some areas another. It may simply be that the bugs in Morocco are different to bugs elsewhere. Whatever the reason, it's best to be cautious about what you buy in both marches centrales and souqs.

A TALE OF TWO SOUQS (URBAN/RURAL)

Fès is the oldest imperial city in Morocco, and one of the most colourful and layered. Steeped in history, the city adheres to a tradition of deep religiosity and boasts a number of exceptional mosques, including the magnificent Karaouine, around which the medina and the extraordinary main souq revolve.

The medina, known as Fès el-Bali, is a honeycomb of some 9400 streets and alleyways. The souq winds around these thoroughfares in a baffling confusion of small shops that, on closer inspection, class themselves by craft according to the guild system. This system has existed here, as in all Moroccan cities, since medieval times. Not much has changed.

Craftsmen carefully hone their wares in front, or in the deep recesses, of their small shops, as they have for generations. People go to the mosque to pray in the same way they have for generations. Fassi cooks hark proudly back to culinary traditions of the 12th and 13th century and are regarded as the purest of traditionalists in the culinary arts. To be born in the old medina of Fès is an esteemed birthright that brings with it a presumption of culture and finesse. Moroccans believe Fassis to be more religious, better cooks, more cultured, refined and artistic than any other identifiable group. Marrying a Fassi woman is said to be a very good thing for a man.

There is no running water in the medina, so inhabitants collect water from wells elaborately decorated with zellig (ceramic tiles often adorning public buildings). No cars are allowed – not that they could possibly pass in the melee – so donkeys make their way through the crowds carting improbable loads up and down the streets. They wear special shoes made of old tyres to help them come to grips with the hilly terrain. The donkey owners shout "Barek!" as a warning to pedestrians, a cry that catalyses a mass pedestrian shift to the sides of the narrow streets.

There are a number of entries to the medina but our favourite for viewing food souqs is the gate near the Place er Rsif. Plunge in.

From the horn-honking, car-ridden dustiness of the place you will immediately enter the exotic half-light of a **qissarya** (covered souq). There is something mythical in the movement from the glaring light and blaring noise of the square down into the narrow, darkened alleyways of the market underworld. We notice a vendor selling French chewing gum, Chuppa Chups, a variety of nuts, sausages and, one suspects, anything else he could get his hands on. As you step down into the souq you'll see all sorts of things – lots of fruit and vegetables, some with little signs giving prices, some without. It's May and wild artichokes are plentiful. You may see calves' feet at the butchers, some stomach-turning intestinal loops, as well as slabs of bleeding meat. A little, heavily veiled lady sells pancakes. Heaped dates, heaped nuts, heaped olives. Live chickens squawk in crates, indignantly awaiting their fate. Have you ever heard a chicken's head cut off, literally in mid-squawk? You may do here. In the meantime, the vendor washes his hands and a rooster flaps pompously on an overhead perch, unaware of the futility of his preening.

As you walk out into the full glare of the street, the smell of cooking meat and a cloud of smoke herald the meat grillers. Meat cooks deliciously and plentifully. A small laiterie sells Orangina, milk drinks, home-made yoghurt and the ubiquitous Coca-Cola. Further on in a small square, more wild artichoke sellers have set up baskets in a circle. One has diversified into zucchinis. Eventually fruit and vegetables give way to copper pots and saucepans, and on it goes.

Another food lover's heaven is to be found to the right of the entrance at Bab Bou Jeloud. The sharp, fresh smell of the citrus juice stand will lead you to another covered souq where foods vie for attention. A fishmonger displays rows of baleful, staring shad from the local river – a good bet if you want fresh fish, as fish imported from the coast is often not the freshest.

There's no floor plan to the souq in Fès, because no plan would ever work. The streets and squares and corners and dead ends are so mind-wrenchingly complex that no plan would ever be purposeful. You would spend more time trying to understand the plan than observing the sights and colours around you.

So, in the absence of any map to the maze, how do you find your way around? Hiring a guide is a good idea, especially for your inaugural dip in the souqs. Guides can be had from the tourist office, or found hanging out near any of the entrances to the medina. They should have official guide badges which carry an official stamp and date with a government insignia. Pick one, work out the price (the tourist office will give you an idea of the going rate) and firmly tell him what you expect to see, and most importantly, what you want to buy. Most guides have deals going with the local vendors and will take you to a series of these shops; however, bargaining is still brisk. You may receive some help from the guide, and it is easier than going it alone, even if you suspect that you are paying a little more at times. Remember, you are under no obligation to buy anything. You may then feel more comfortable going back alone other times. Your other option is to try and negotiate the twists and turns yourself, but don't blame anyone if you get lost.

The souqs of the major cities of Fès, Marrakesh, Casablanca and Rabat are more or less similar in the exuberant array of goods and foods for sale. The smaller souqs of the countryside are much simpler.

Middle Atlas Souq

Throughout rural Morocco, for one day each week, souqs transform normally sedate villages into mini festivals. As the surrounding rural population converges – by the busload, in cars, trucks and taxis, some by donkey, others by mule and cart – it provides a day for meeting and for making friends, and perhaps even finding a marriage partner. More mundanely, it's also an opportunity to take advantage of the town's services, to carry out administrative chores and pay bills. Out of towners buy meat and get cafes to cook it for them, eating outside in groups. You may not want to buy anything at these souqs, but they make for a fascinating wander, for the people-watching as much as the produce.

In Zaouit Cheikh, you know it's Wednesday when you see a man walking down the street casually dangling two live chickens by their feet. As we keep walking, the streets fill, and when we come to the normally quiet intersection, its cafes are bursting with men, pedestrians have overtaken the road, and the beggar with the ulcerated leg is displaying it to his best advantage. Though the weekly souq finishes around dusk, the best action is in the morning when the superior fruit and vegetables are sold – poor people buy up the cheap leftovers in the afternoon.

This is a conservative town, but on Wednesdays it feels like it has been thrust back to the Middle Ages. Raggedly turbaned Berber men ride past on their donkeys, and old Berber women with blue tattooed chins shuffle past with white cotton lengths of cloth draped over their heads and bodies. As ever in Morocco, the antique and the modern provide startling contrasts: a stall selling the latest sports clothes vies with one featuring woven saddle-baskets for donkeys, some of which are tethered contentedly together under a knot of shady trees.

Under awnings, a row of barbers shave the heads of old Berber men. Live chickens stare across feather-strewn ground to the stall selling eggs, and smaller growers use their donkey's saddle-baskets to display their produce, perching cross-legged behind their wares, mint tea in progress. Huge mounds of tomatoes, apples, oranges, purple onions and bright yellow melons are spread colourfully on the ground. Piles of green herbs – the essential mint, coriander, and parsley – are fragrant in the hot sun. Vendors cry out their wares – "**Rabaja**!" (Here are cheap things), "**Reclame, reclame**!" (Discount, discount!), "**Agilana**!" (Come here!), "**Lem are lee haina**" (I have the best here), while one uses a loudspeaker to attract attention to his pile of peanuts.

Savoury smelling smoke wafts from beneath an open tent where flattened keftas are being grilled over a fire. You can eat the simple fare with bread and mint tea. Elsewhere there's fish frying in a pan, with the typical accompaniments of sliced fried eggplant, grilled green capsicums, and a salad of tomato, onion and coriander. A corn seller offers some of his grill-blackened cobs, while the cactus look-alike hindir (prickly pear), is being prepared. A roving water-seller – in traditional colourful costume and huge hat – dispenses water in bronze drinking cups for Dr1.

Our baskets fill with purplish-red, round **rammahn** (pomegranate), pears and lemons too, and we choose from the wooden boxes of red and black grapes. We leave the piles of green herbs until last, moving on to relieve the tables groaning under flat round woven baskets displaying a variety of dates, and strings of figs. We buy some black-roasted sunflower seeds and carefully crack them between our teeth. Later, we'll chew some small sticks of arach wood from the Sahara, which will brighten our teeth. The wood sits next to piles of dried henna leaves, which I had only seen before as a green powder. My friends tell me we can even eat the summer fruit of the tree, leading me to an old man sitting in front of a pile of the round brown marble-sized fruit called nbeg, unable to help himself from occasionally eating into his profits. We buy some, and eat only the chalky outer layer, throwing away the hard core to be trodden into the rubbish strewn ground as we walk away from the throng.

Margo Daly

Street souk, Fès

Types of Shops

In the larger souqs, shops are small partitioned rooms lining the streets. They're usually filled to the rafters with the produce they offer for sale. In Marrakesh, some food vendors have built pitched structures for their wares so that all is visible from the street – the vendor sits in a tiny space in the middle where he can access anything he has for sale.

Epiceries

The equivalent of the corner store, epiceries are found throughout Morocco. They were introduced during the French occupation, hence the name. These are mini-supermarkets and stock anything from toothpaste to toilet paper, milk to wine. They will sometimes also have olives, spices, fruit, vegetables and other traditional food as well as exotic imported food, usually tinned. They always stock sweets of various types. Naturally, some epiceries are better than others. Good ones will be constantly busy and boast refrigeration of some sort. The bad ones inevitably have faded and flyblown chewing gum in the window and not a lot of stock. Some enterprising owners have set up fax and photocopying machines as well.

In terms of alcohol, the limits are vague; some sell it all the time, others have set hours. It depends on the shopkeeper, it seems. The rule with epiceries is that if this one doesn't have it, another will. Epiceries in the countryside may also be cafes, or even restaurants.

Souq Epiceries

These are proto-epiceries that grow like clusters of mushrooms along some of the souq streets. Unlike epiceries proper, they don't sell a wide range of goods. Usually they stock a few disparate things without much rhyme or reason. It may be sauce, cigarettes and olives; or it may be chewing gum, a feeble selection of sweets, and some warm cans of Coke.

Hypermarches

Morocco seems to have jumped the supersouq barrier to arrive straight at the hypersouq. Situated on the outskirts of the major towns, the hypermarches are just like anywhere else in the world – large emporia of goods surrounded by huge carparks. In Morocco the specials bins are full of imitation rugs and **babouches** (slippers), there is a large aisle devoted to sugar cones, and the meat is halal (killed according to Islamic law). Packaged cakes, a large stock of wines and beer, frozen foods, and tinned foods abound – these are the same the world over. Surrounding the central supersouq section are a series of smaller boutiques selling such things as shoes, clothes and fast food. Pizza Hut is a favourite lessee of these halls.

Marches Centrales
These souqs are found in most of the new towns of the major cities and are useful as one-stop shops for all sorts of Moroccan foods. They are usually predominantly food oriented, unlike the more general souqs of the medina. The food is just as good, if not markedly better, than that found in the souqs. Bargaining is not as brisk, making for more relaxed shopping, and they are less confusing. Usually housed in a large warehouse or custom built buildings, the marches centrales are more modern than the souqs, but still sell goods in the same way with similar set ups.

Butchers
Meat is suspended from hooks over the counter and arranged in displays behind. Heads, feet and intestines are sometimes showcased. Sometimes the meat is garlanded with fine white cheesecloth to keep flies away. Theoretically, meat is sold within the day, although sometimes this seems a dubious claim.

Poulterers
Chickens are kept live in crates to be killed as required. Some sophisticated poulterers will have plucking machines, others do the deed over a drum of charcoals which singes the feathers off.

Patisseries
Here you'll find Moroccan cakes and biscuits. Patisseries are common in the souqs and the new towns, where they closely follow the French model, and offer both Moroccan and European delicacies. In the souqs, you can buy pastries from many street vendors and in shops selling sweetmeats.

Often, the sweet stuff is put into decorative packages wrapped with cellophane and ribbons to give as gifts and, as such, they are perfect for that invitation to a Moroccan home.

Trolleys & Crates
Apart from the small shops, souqs are punctuated with vendors selling their wares from little trolleys, or even small crates and boxes placed strategically along your path. These vendors are usually selling whatever it is that they have brought in from the country. Sometimes however, they can be locals, who don't happen to have a shop. Lacking a formal outlet, they simply set up in a good position and offer whatever it is that they have for sale – bread, eggs, chicks, a turkey or two, fresh goats cheese, fresh farm honey, slabs of nougat, seasonal vegetables such as wild artichokes or asparagus, or baskets of live snails.

Traiteurs

These are mostly found in the new parts of town, and offer freshly prepared and cooked food from a display counter. It is the perfect marriage of Moroccan food with a French way of doing things. Traiteurs are particularly useful if you want to take food on the road between stops; or simply to pick up a small cup of olives to nibble as you walk. They are especially good when you want to go back to your hotel and eat well of the local produce, without having to eat out.

Laiteries

In some areas, you may find a laiterie, a French word meaning a shop selling milk products. These shops, in fact, sell all sorts of refrigerated drinks including soft drinks and milk drinks. They sell home-made yoghurt in little jars and, sometimes, sweet rice puddings.

Wild artichokes, Fès

Fruit & Vegetables

Some shops offer a wide range of produce, including spices. Others specialise in seasonal produce at competitive prices.

Nuts, Pulses & Dried Fruit

These foods are sold in various combinations, piled in tubs, much like spices. The range depends on the season to some extent, although chickpeas, walnuts, dates, figs and apricots seem to be produced pretty much all year round. These products are sold by specialist vendors but can also be found with fruit and spice vendors within the souq.

Olives & Preserves

Heaped in tubs, olives and preserved lemons make one of the most attractive displays at the souq. A range of olives is usually presented in every hue both plain and with sharmoola or harissa dressings. Diced vegetable preserves are sometimes shown in tubs, sometimes in glass jars, always pretty to look at.

Preserved olives and lemons, Meknès

Herbs & Spices

Mint and coriander are usually sold in generous bunches from trolleys or specialist vendors, who sell nothing but these fragrant herbs. Otherwise, they're sold at fruit & vegetable vendors, and less often, at the spice shop. The richly coloured and scented spices are piled high in tubs and sold by weight – Moroccan housewives tend to buy less and more often, as they are rigorous about the freshness of their condiments. Spice shops are often also pharmacies, and vice versa – in this case, all sorts of strange, gnarled roots and colourful berries are on offer, as well as the odd chameleon (who eats flies and insects), or lizards live or stiffly dead (to ward off the evil eye).

Pots & Pans

Apart from the huge range of other handicrafts, Moroccans make some excellent pots and pans with and without copper. Craftsmen display their goods in a glittering tumble outside shops, or carefully place a series of impressively enormous pieces in view of the passer-by. You'll also often see the series of connected metal balls used to adorn the top of mosques, which are also made here. Also look for **siniyya**, the magnificent chased copper trays complete with fold-out wooden support, that enable them to turn into side tables. And don't forget teaware; pots, trays and tea boxes.

Tajines & Pottery

Tajines are found all over Morocco in various shops, including general household goods shops, and are sold in various shapes and sizes, often with their braziers underneath. You'll also find them sold in pottery shops along with more ornate pottery ware used for display rather than for cooking.

Household Goods

These shops tend to carry everything for the home, from crockery to plastic ware to pottery. In particular, these shops offer a wide range of the glasses used by Moroccans to drink their tea.

Embroidery Shops

Filled with the work of nimble Moroccan fingers, these shops are found in most large souqs. Fine embroidery has a long tradition in Morocco and no self-respecting household would set the table with anything less. Nowadays, embroidered napkins are also available.

Basketry & Utensils

Many of the traditional utensils of Moroccan food preparation are made from basket weave including beautifully decorated wide, shallow receptacles, bread 'tajines' and other small baskets. Wooden utensils such as spoons and forks are also sold in basket weave shops.

The Pharmacy

Pharmacies are usually narrow walk-in shops as opposed to stalls on the street. As you walk past walls lined with glass jars full of ingredients, you may see the odd eye of newt, foot of frog or other odd dried concoctions. Pharmacists will make up any medicine to suit your ailment, even if you're lovesick. They'll happily list the ingredients of each remedy but when you ask about the cures for being lovestruck, or medicines to alleviate evil eye symptoms, they always become suave and secretive.

Baskets for sale, Salè

Things to Take Home

Don't forget to purchase a large woven shopping basket – these come in all shapes and sizes, are very strong and last for years. Other items to look for include the wonderful and sometimes ornately-woven bread holders and placemats, good for placing hot dishes such as tajines directly onto the table for serving. Tajines are a particularly good item to put on the shopping list, along with the vast array of richly decorative pottery items for serving nuts, salads, and the larger dishes that serve as exotic fruit bowls. Include the heavily embroidered tablecloths, napkins, ornate copper and silver-plated serving ware and you have a table setting fit for a Sultan. Enjoy your very own mint tea and perfect the technique with a Moroccan tea pot and embellished glasses. Set the scene with forged iron lamps and mosaic-tiled zellig tables, while you settle back on cushions woven by Berber hill tribes.

Foodstuffs are more difficult. Check with customs before you go – you may be able to bring spices back although, remember, Moroccans buy spices in small quantities as needed.

where to eat & drink

Moroccans rarely dine out – to do so would be a slight on the cooking of their mother or wife which, of course, is the best. Therefore, the restaurant scene is almost exclusively for tourists, travellers and Moroccans on the road. Even so, restaurants provide a good introduction to Moroccan cuisine, and the street food will always add some colourful atmosphere to your dining experience.

Traditionally, socialising in Morocco takes place within the confines of the home. Eating out, in the sense of going to restaurants, is very much the reserve of the new urban generation, who are less tied to the family and more to the work place. Workers will sometimes eat out at a cafe or pizzeria for lunch rather than returning home, especially if home is far away. In the evening pizzerias are favourite places for courting couples to pursue some discreet billing and cooing. Taboos against women and any overt courtship are very strong – it wouldn't be good for an unmarried girl's reputation to be seen in too independent a situation. The pizzerias are homely and safe.

In rural Morocco, festivals and special events are occasions for celebratory intra-village feasts, but the concept of restaurants is virtually unknown. Many larger villages will have a bar or cafe where men can congregate, but apart from the roadside stops, restaurants are uncommon.

Moroccans sometimes eat out *en famille* at the fish markets in port areas. After all, eating grilled fish straight from the boat is different. However they'd rarely choose a restaurant serving Moroccan food. Why bother with a stranger's food for which you have to pay? Moroccan etiquette demands that food be given to any visitor, so the idea of a restaurant serving Moroccan food for payment doesn't sit well with some people.

Moroccan travellers – anyone on the move – eat at roadside cafes catering specifically to people in transit. However, if a friend or relative lives

HIDDEN COSTS

Tax should be included in the final cost of your bill and in the cost of the items as they appear on your menu. Tipping is up to you – there is no set rule and no set expectation.

You may run into trouble sometimes in hotels. Some charge a rate for half-pension, others for full. If you're on half-pension, you may be charged an exorbitant amount for an evening meal because they often only offer a full buffet. Or, you may be paying for lunch, included in the room price, even though you have no intention of eating lunch in the hotel. Check how the system works before signing in. Also check the policy on room service and avoid any check-out surprises.

Also, remember to check the drink prices in the bars of hotels. Otherwise, your hangover could be worse than you bargained for. Most hotels – really the only places to drink alcohol comfortably in this teetotal country – charge the customer quite a lot for the privilege of imbibing.

in the town through which they are passing, then they'll almost certainly eat there.

Moroccan restaurants range from lavish affairs – servicing tourists and important guests – in cities and large towns to simple roadside stops, catering for anyone passing through. Some of the larger hotels incorporate a special Moroccan-style restaurant showcasing local cuisine. Other restaurants provide international fare.

Street stall, Place Djemaa el Fna, Marrakesh

Undeniably, the best culinary experience you're likely to have in Morocco is a family dinner at someone's house. If you've met people on the road who invite you to share a meal, a small cash remuneration, graciously and discreetly given, is often appreciated. However if they are friends, or friends of friends, make sure you bring a gift, as offering money could be regarded as an indignity.

مقهى
CAFE

Where to Eat

Despite the formal lack of a restaurant tradition among Moroccans, enterprise prevails. This is, after all, an Arab country where commercial opportunities are exploited in full. Consequently, wherever there are tourists or visitors, food will be available. The way in which you choose to eat depends on budget and location. While in larger towns and cities there are eateries to suit a wide range of budgets and preferences, smaller towns and villages may be more restricted.

Lunch is the major meal for Moroccans, and while larger establishments and hotels will serve full-scale dinners, you might prefer to alter your habits to suit Moroccan time. The midday meal is an important affair and, while the country doesn't necessarily shut down, things do *slow* down.

One way or another, there are ample means to get your daily feed, from the simplest street vendor to the most elaborate and highly serviced restaurant combining all the best of the gracious Moroccan tradition with the efficiency of modern cooking methods and service.

Cutlery and napkins are usually available in Morocco, although locals may eat with their hands. Do what feels best.

Restaurants

Moroccan restaurants are the obvious choice for visitors, and there are some impressive examples throughout the country. Most of these will be elaborately decorated in the Moroccan style. Some of the best ones (notably Yacout in Marrakesh and La Maison Bleue in Fès) are magnificently reworked renditions of small private palaces. Restaurants typically offer a full range of Moroccan-style fare – tajines, couscous, **brochettes** (kebabs), salads, desserts. Many are also licensed.

Prices can be relatively high, although compared to similar dining experiences elsewhere, they're not expensive. The food is generally very good, with even the top restaurants employing a bevy of local women in the kitchens.

Some restaurants take the picturesque theme to extravagant lengths. You may be treated to roving bands of musicians, dancing girls, fantasias (the charge of young would-be warriors on their decorative horses), snake charmers and even belly dancing. Most of the belly-dancers are imported from Egypt, and while they are inevitably gorgeous and sinuous, they are not part of the Moroccan tradition. However, don't let that prevent you enjoying the show. Gnaoua bands (identified by their shell-encrusted hats and rhythmic, haunting singing) from the Saharan regions and players of flute and **ud** (similar to the mandolin) are genuinely Moroccan, and provide a seductive aural backdrop in the better restaurants.

Entrance to Cafe Maure, overlooking the sea, Rabat

Hotels

The better hotels in Morocco always have a restaurant in-house. Some of them are among the best in the country. Hotel restaurants sometimes treat the method of cooking slightly differently due to the vast quantities of food required and means of storage they employ. However, while the head chefs may be European in origin, the kitchens are really run by women, who cook in the traditional way. By common consent, no one else really knows how to do it.

Palais de Fès

Cafes

Small cafes abound. They serve breakfasts, lunches and dinners, with the size and sophistication of the establishment determining the type and quality of food available. Some will offer Moroccan specialities – a tajine or two, brochettes, perhaps couscous – as well as general Mediterranean dishes such as composed salads and the ubiquitous pizzas or chips. For breakfast you may find **baguettes** (long bread rolls), Moroccan pancakes or simple bread, butter and jam. Mint tea and coffee are always on offer.

Cafes are generally open early enough for breakfast. Many of them close at around 6pm although some are also open for dinner. It's common practice to bring your own croissants and cakes from local **patisseries** (pastry shops).

Catching up, Marrakesh

Roadside Stops

Drive-in roadside stops are built along all the major roads of Morocco. They are typically long, low cement buildings, quite shabby and often incorporating a small mosque. A series of small shops opens out onto a porch along which chairs and tables are ranged. Cars, trucks and other vehicles line up in the car park in front of the building. Typically, visitors first choose meat from the samples on offer, which is then grilled in brochettes or **kefta** (minced meat) balls, minced on the spot, and served with salads and bread. Tajines are usually available, lined up in picturesque serried ranks. Small cafes sell drinks and takeaway food and you'll also find fruit and vegetables, as these roadside conglomerations often attract local farmers selling their wares.

Menus

Your menu will depend entirely on the type of restaurant you're in – some smaller restaurants or cafes may not even have one, the dish of the day being the entire list. If cafes offer a menu it's usually sectioned simply according to the drinks and snacks on offer. Where the menu is small or non-existent, it's always worth asking if there's anything else apart from the specials.

Most menus are in French and, increasingly, in English. Arabic menus are extremely rare. Remember, the idea of eating out is very much an introduced custom to the Moroccans and menus are tailored to cater for foreign visitors.

The French terms for Moroccan food are very similar to English translations. Entree is, of course, **entree** (starter). **Plat principal** means main course, although the menu usually heads this section with tajines and/or couscous – the same in both languages. Dessert is also the same. For reference, meat in French is **viande**, chicken is **poulet** and fish is **poisson**. Vegetables are **legumes**.

Central Market, Fès

Reading the Menu

Once you have grasped the basic terms of Moroccan cuisine, reading the menu is simple. As you travel throughout the country you'll notice that most restaurants offer a selection of dishes around the same themes. These themes are typically Moroccan – salads, tajines, couscous, **bastila** (pigeon or poultry pie), as well as desserts.

The a la carte menu usually lists the salads first (possibly as entrees), sometimes including a few soups, then tajines and couscous. Salads tend to be offered as a selection. Tajines generally cover all options from lamb to chicken, beef and possibly fish, with a selection of accompanying vegetables. Couscous is usually lamb or chicken with vegetables, although there are some variations.

Desserts aren't important in traditional Moroccan cuisine but they will turn up on menus (for the tourists). Fruits are a big favourite, and will be found in most eateries.

For breakfast, most of the large hotels offer a buffet-style selection covering the gamut of tourist preferences from traditional English bacon and eggs, baguettes and croissants and **brioche** (breakfast pastries) to Moroccan pancakes with honey and butter. Cafes will typically offer a simpler range. Otherwise, toasted Moroccan bread with jam or honey is ubiquitous.

Only the most tourist-oriented restaurants will give a comprehensive rundown of ingredients. This doesn't necessarily mean that the restaurant is a tourist trap – remember that many restaurants owe their existence to tourists and do their best to accommodate them. Menus don't usually state whether a dish is vegetarian or not. Even if you order a couscous with vegetables only, check what sort of stock is used. Some restaurants will offer a vegetarian tajine but you should ask about the ingredients to make sure.

Moroccan food is rarely hot but a few dishes do use chilli. These will be marked on the menu. Harissa, the hot spicy condiment made with crushed chillies, is usually served as a side dish, so the choice is yours.

Set menus are common, often as an alternative to the a la carte fare. The selection typically includes salads, a tajine and/or couscous, followed by a dessert (bastila or sometimes a foreign interloper such as chocolate mousse or creme caramel) or fruit. Meals are always finished with coffee or tea.

Drinks are usually in a separate section of the menu. Alcohol is available in hotel restaurants of any standing. Non-alcoholic drinks include freshly squeezed juices, almond milk and of course, mineral water. Some restaurants serve a cocktail of freshly squeezed orange juice with a few drops of orange flower water. As a starter, there are few drinks more refreshing to the palate.

Vegetarians & Vegans

Because of the rich proliferation of salads and vegetables in Moroccan food, vegetarians and vegans will be able to enjoy a great deal of the Moroccan culinary experience without compromise.

Cooked vegetable salads are the best bet – although vegans need to watch out for the occasional addition of **smen**, a form of butter (see Smen under Butter & Yoghurt in the Staples & Specialities chapter). Sometimes vegetable tajines are on the menu, but beware of the stock in which they're cooked – it may well be meat-based. Couscous with fava beans is a simple dish that's easy to make (if fava beans are not in season then dried fava beans will do). If you're demi-veg, fish tajines or grilled fish aren't too hard to track down, particularly in coastal areas. Shellfish are not usually included in Moroccan dishes unless stated, and then, only in fish dishes.

Vegans may have to live entirely on salads, pulses and fruit – not such a bad option in Morocco.

Bear in mind that Moroccans really have no concept of vegetarianism. You may find yourself repeating constantly what vegetarian means and why you don't eat meat.

Like many peasant-based cuisines, vegetables are commonly used in Moroccan dishes but meat is prized for its protein-giving qualities as well as flavour. Even when vegetables are the only ingredients available, most Moroccans will endeavour to add some form of meat. Only when there is no meat available can you be assured that the dish is completely vegetarian, in which case protein-rich pulses such as chickpeas are used in its place. Vegetables do form an important part of dishes but rarely on their own.

Grilling peppers to remove skins

Children

Remember that it's most unusual for Moroccans to take children out to restaurants, so there are no specific accommodations made for them. However, Moroccans adore children and are generally happy to oblige with any special requirements.

The major issue with feeding children may well be the generally spicy nature of Moroccan food – while it's rarely spicy hot, the richness of the spices may cause upset. On the other hand, the communal nature of Moroccan dining, and the prospect of eating with hands, may be very appealing to the young ones and they can have hours of messy fun. Trying to keep to the right hand rule may be difficult to impose, but most Moroccans are quite indulgent with youngsters, so a fair effort will be appreciated and failure overlooked.

Watch for nuts in some dishes and pastries if your child is too young to digest them properly.

Children will love the wide availability of fizzy drinks and probably the sweet mint tea too, although parents may have to deal with the fall-out from sugar hits.

LOW BROW SNACKS

Sweets and western-style snack foods are on the up in Morocco, and have become an integral part of the street food mix. Chips, ice creams, candy bars, chewing gum, mints, lollipops, or any other small, desirably packaged items are increasingly part of the everyday.

Ice creams are usually sold by vendors from portable or lockable freezers emblazoned with the insignia of (usually) French ice cream manufacturers, who must be thrilled to have found another outlet for their sticky offerings.

Candy bars and chips among other things, are sold at newspaper stands, tobacconists, **epiceries** (general stores) and drink stalls. For those addicted to their daily fix of chocolate or sugary sweet, no abstinence is necessary as sweets are everywhere.

For the multi-cultural sweet tooth, some of the local brands are well worth trying. Packaged in cellophane and ribbon, or bought by weight in slabs, Moroccan nougat will give you just what the pretty pastel colours suggest: a sugary sweet hit with a slightly sickly aftertaste. Just what every sweetaholic needs to stop eating more. More refined biscuits and sweetmeats can be bought from the patisserie, or the sweet shops in the souq.

ETHNIC CUISINE

While French culinary habits may have influenced the local cuisine, there are surprisingly few restaurants serving Gallic fare. The best French food is usually found in the hotels where chefs are French. Some French restaurants do exist in each city, as signalled by their French names. The menu and execution are generally authentic.

Moroccans are fascinated by Chinese and Vietnamese food, and you'll find restaurants in major cities and towns. The oriental attraction to spices has obvious similarities to Moroccan cuisine, although one sophisticated Moroccan confided that Chinese food was too spicy for his taste. Most Moroccans secretly believe that their own cuisine is second to none, but are quite receptive to the novelty of Chinese and Vietnamese food.

Pizzerias proliferate and can be found flourishing in the centre of major cities and towns. The pizza combination of a bread base and rich topping seems to marry well with one important aspect of Moroccan cuisine – that of using bread to pick up food. The mixture of ingredients also appeals to the Moroccans, who are used to eating multi-ingredient tajines and couscous.

Pizzas are cheap and favoured by the young, who congregate in pizzerias in well-behaved clusters. You'll often hear music, modern Moroccan or Algerian as well as western favourites. Pizza Hut is making inroads into Moroccan culinary life, often placed strategically in the large hypermarches. These outlets are usually a bit more expensive than local pizzerias, selling on the idea of genuine American fast food, which holds a certain cachet. Pizzerias sometimes offer pasta dishes as well.

Other fast food such as hamburgers and chips are sometimes sold at **friteries** (fried food shops) or pizzerias. The hamburgers often have the distinctly Moroccan flavour of cumin and paprika, and the bun is often Moroccan bread (better than the imported buns that fail to please by any standards). Chips and tomato sauce are the same the world over.

Where to Drink

There are some bars in Morocco, frequented only by men. Foreign males may be welcome but women are not. These bars are usually small holes in the wall in the souqs or, more often, in the new parts of towns. There are strict laws prohibiting alcohol in the medina in Fés.

Drinking alcohol is more common in hotels. Most three-star hotels serve booze, which can be taken with food at dinner or in a hotel bar. Foreign women in groups or accompanied by a male are tolerated. Single women – even if they are foreign – are mostly presumed to be prostitutes.

Street Food

Morocco street food offers the visitor an extraordinary opportunity to experience the authentic tastes and scents of this marvellous cuisine without even sitting down. Before trying food from the streets and **souqs** (markets), a few sensible warnings should be taken into consideration.

Firstly, beware of bugs. While most street vendors use ingredients that are fresh and healthy – locals would not patronise a vendor who sold food of dubious quality – it is worthwhile being careful. If you're seduced by the delicious aroma of frying meat laced with cumin and other spices – one of the scents always weaving through the souq – but don't trust the meat, it's perfectly acceptable to fetch your own. However, compared to the cumin-scented grill, the aroma of the meat market might just banish your appetite.

Obviously, go with the crowds. If locals are patronising one seller over another, then there is usually a good reason. High turnover is a good indicator of fresh and unsullied produce.

Having said this, freshness is something that all Moroccans insist upon. Apart from this tenet, there are simply too many vendors selling the same produce for bad food to be commercially viable (except, perhaps, in the poorest of farflung outposts). In fact, street food may well be fresher than that served in restaurants and cafes, as it is cooked at the point of sale. It's certainly much cheaper.

Apart from these rules, eating in the souqs is simple. If you don't like the look or smell of it, don't eat it. If there are no Moroccans buying the stuff, walk on.

What is available to eat in the street markets? Almost everything. From tajines to couscous to grilled kebabs; cooked vegetable salads, preserves such as olives, cheeses and yoghurt, bowls of harira soup, grilled eggplant

PREPARE FOR A GRILLING

The food souqs are redolent with the delicious smell of grilled meats. **Bulfahf** (liver laced with cumin and coarse salt) is popular, and **brochettes** (kebabs) are common offerings. Kefta balls are also a favourite (see Meats in the Staples & Specialities chapter). The meat is grilled over charcoal on skewers, whipped off into a piece of bread, and eaten like a sandwich. In some places you may also get some chips and salad stuffed into the bread envelope, which you can jazz up with a dollop of **harissa** (chilli sauce).

and capsicum, dried fruit and nuts, pots of honey or amelou; even preserved meat and of course, bread.

Pulses such as lentils and chickpeas are often sold from street trolleys – served hot in paper cones and laced with onion and capsicums, cumin and coriander, these snacks are delicious, filling and nourishing. Another variation on this theme is a dish of mashed fava beans served with cumin, red capsicum and olive oil.

For the brave – braver than us – sheep's heads on spits are regarded as a delicacy. Usually served with couscous, they make a gruesome sight but the meat is said to be rich and tender.

Yoghurt is another favourite snack. Bought in small **laiteries** (dairy and soft drink sellers) in glass jars, it's eaten on the spot, standing up, with spoons provided. Yoghurt is usually home-made, and can be sweetened with honey.

Fruit juice is sold from behind counters piled high with bright oranges. Juicing is done on the spot. Some vendors will mix fruits for you, and add a few drops of orange flower water to enhance the flavours. The smaller, brightly coloured oranges are usually sweeter, although all Moroccan oranges seem impregnated with a dose of cheerful, sunlit juiciness.

Dried fruits make an excellent nibble or conclusion to a grill sandwich. Buy a selection of dates, almonds, sunflower seeds and figs for a delicious and fortifying snack.

MARRAKESH FOOD & STREET THEATRE

The food markets of the huge Djemaa el-Fna square in Marrakesh are a street food paradise. Each evening the stalls set up in the centre of the enormous space, fringed with performers of all types – acrobats, story-tellers, fortune tellers, snake charmers, musicians and dancers. The street stalls offer pews on which diners sit to consume their food and watch the show unfold, while water sellers wade colourfully through the throng. Soup, grilled meat, salads, hot tubs of chickpeas, chips, fish, even snails – you can find anything. Choose whatever you want, then sit and watch it being prepared. For a minimal fee you can eat your fill in the centre of this magnificent street theatre.

Fish cafe, Essaouira

2750

A Moroccan Picnic

Picnicking, as most of us know it, is not common among Moroccans, and many will be mystified by the concept of taking off somewhere just for the pleasure of eating outdoors. However, this shouldn't stop you from enjoying your own DIY dining experience, and a visit to the souq will furnish you with all you need for your Moroccan picnic.

Moroccan roads have many beautiful picnic sites along them. The road between Rabat and Fès in the Khemisset region, for example, offers many marvellous views. If you're trekking, the walk up from Imlil to Asni offers stunning views and, at this altitude, there are still plenty of trees under which you can sit. You may be lucky – as we were – to run into some women collecting sticks, who will surely share their tea with you.

It's in the mountains that you will be able to really do things Moroccan style, although you'll need to buy meat and carry it, so don't expect to go too far. Firstly build a campfire. Over this, you can grill brochettes or kefta, which can be bought from the butcher, complete with a marinade

PICNIC & THE PORTABLE STOVE

Kefta, the delicious casserole of meatballs in a curry-like sauce, is one of the simplest and quickest tajines to make, and perfect for a roadside picnic. En route to Marrakesh, we stopped by a line of shady Saf Saf trees, spread out a blanket, and Hassan produced the essential portable stove. His family has a stack of these and they really come into their own on hot summer nights when the whole family encamps to the spacious rooftop of their house in the Middle Atlas – cooking, eating, taking tea, sleeping, even watching television under the stars. The Moroccan love of outdoor living reaches its peak in August, as whole tent cities erect themselves anywhere remotely scenic.

Margo Daly

Fishing boats, Taghazout, Atlantic Coast

of cumin and salt. If the fish in the market looks good, you could try that instead. Buy a lemon for flavour, or rub a **sharmoola** (marinade) into the flesh before you leave.

If you find a good traiteur in the market, you'll be able to buy a selection of salads or cold meats.

In any event, bread is essential. You may want to dip the bread into Moroccan olive oil, which can be purchased at the epicerie or some of the vegetable vendors. You may even pass olive oil vendors on the side of the road – they herald their goods by tying a bunch of colourful plastic bottles together on a tree like balloons. From the market or from the country oil vendors you'll be able to buy olives – the market will offer a broader selection with a wider range of treatments.

Cakes or biscuits can be found in the market or in the patisseries of the new towns. You may find honey sold on the farms – or buy it from the vendors at the market. Most epiceries sell honey.

Another crucial element is tea. You may want to make the tea over the fire with a teapot and glasses bought for a few dirham in the market. In this case, remember to bring some Chinese tea as well as sugar and a large bunch of mint. If you're picnicking in one of the parks found in the major towns, it might be good idea to reconvene to the nearest congenial cafe and take tea there.

a moroccan banquet

Once you return from Morocco, it won't be long before you experience a nostalgic yearning for rich, fragrant spices. Fortunately, Moroccan food can be simple to prepare and there are a few steps you can take to reproduce the whole experience. If you're a Moroccan food aficionado, you should definitely try the banquet dish par excellence, **bastila** (pigeon or poultry pie).

Moroccan food is convivial by nature, and best experienced in warm and happy company. Try eating with your hands in the traditional Arab style. If your guests are willing, explain the rules; right hand, only three fingers and no licking of fingers until the end of the meal.

Start with a mint tea ceremony. You may not be able to get the cones of sugar you became fond of in Morocco but fine white sugar is a good substitute. If you forgot to buy a Moroccan tea pot, a standard one will do. Serve some of those tiny biscuits so loved by Moroccans, even if guests – accustomed to *savoury* titbits before a meal – are a little non-plussed. If you're drinking wine, save the tea ceremony until after the meal and offer some savoury chips or nuts that, while not very traditional, are still in keeping with the theme. Just call chips 'modern Moroccan' – a lot of shops in the **medinas** (old quarters) of Morocco serve piles of chips, and Moroccans seem to have taken to this import.

Bastila, see recipe on next page

A round table is best for conversation and access to the main dishes but, for a touch of authenticity, lay a cloth on the floor and surround it with cushions. This is particularly good if you're eating with your hands.

How much food you prepare depends on time, budget and number of guests, but remember the amount of food at a Moroccan banquet usually far outweighs the number of guests. You may want to reduce the amount, particularly as you (probably) won't have an army of veiled cooks in the kitchen ready to devour the leftovers. Many a Moroccan banquet has taken place outside of Morocco with a single main dish as the centrepiece – couscous is a favourite – although serious cooks who have the time will want to showcase two or three.

A house, Essaouira

Bastila

Bastila is not so much difficult to prepare as time consuming. It requires a degree of concentration that most other Moroccan recipes do not, although it is one of the flagship Moroccan dishes that you should try at least once.

Ingredients

1kg	pastry leaves (filo or spring-roll pastry will do)
2	chickens or 12 pigeons
1kg	onions
20	eggs
500g	blanched almonds
1	bunch of parsley
1	pinch of saffron, pulverised from threads
3	teaspoons ginger
1	teaspoon pepper
3	teaspoons cinnamon
2	sticks of cinnamon
1kg	butter
1	cup sugar
	salt to taste

Cooking the Chicken or Pigeons

Put the grated onions, chopped parsley, salt, saffron, ginger, pepper, cinnamon sticks, 750g of the butter and a glass of water into a pot. As soon as the mixture starts to boil, add the poultry with the gizzards and let cook. If necessary, add water during cooking. When the poultry is cooked, take out of the pot.

Take all the meat from the bones and cut it very finely. Discard the bones and reduce the stock remaining in the pot into a sauce.

Preparing the Stuffing of Eggs & Onions

Whisk 18 of the eggs and add them to the reduced sauce. Add half the sugar and let the mixture cook while gently stirring. When the mixture congeals like scrambled eggs, take the pot off the stove and leave to one side.

Preparing the Almonds

Fry the almonds in a little oil until golden. Strain them, and put through a blender until minced finely. Add the rest of the sugar to the almond mix.

Composition of the Dish

Cover the bottom of a wide, shallow dish with leaves of pastry, leaving enough to come up over the edges. Whisk the remaining two eggs, and paint the leaves to bind them together while cooking. As this layer forms the base of the pie, add a few more leaves to the centre of the dish and paint them also. Put a layer of egg stuffing and then a layer of almond mixture over the base. Add another layer of pastry leaves in the same manner. Add a layer of chopped poultry meat, sprinkling any liquid from the egg stuffing over it. Use all the chopped poultry meat for this layer.

Repeat a layer of pastry leaves, and another layer of egg stuffing and almond mixture. Finally, lay the last layer of pastry leaves on top. Remember to always paint each layer of pastry with the egg mixture.

Put the pie in a medium oven and let the top brown gently. Before serving, add a little butter to the top, and then sprinkle a liberal amount of powdered sugar and cinnamon over the top. Traditionally, the two are sprinkled in a crisscross pattern.

Serve the dish hot. If you're eating it with your hands – the traditional way – plunge your fingers into the pie. It can also be cut into wedges and served on plates.

Serves 12

A couple of cooked salads and bread should form the entree although, if you want to simplify proceedings, they can be served with the couscous or tajine. Follow the Moroccan preference for dessert – a range of fresh fruits, perhaps served with dried fruit and nuts. Make sure there is plenty of bread and finish your meal with tea.

While in Morocco, get some cassettes or CDs of local musicians. At the shops selling music in the souq, you can listen before you buy. Cassettes can be bought for a few dirham, and are easy to carry home. Gnaoua music is a traditional favourite, and the compelling rhythms and singing are an excellent backdrop to a Moroccan meal. Music featuring the **ud** is also suitable; the gentle, woody tones of this instrument are seductive and calming. Moroccans also like to listen to Egyptian belly dancing music – in the absence of a belly dancer you may find that some of your guests will oblige – and **raï**, the modern Algerian form of dance music. Raï can be heard in clubs all over the world now, and is guaranteed to get everyone up and dancing. Cheb Khaled is the most popular exponent.

Good wine, good food and good music is always a winning combination. Your guests couldn't ask for anything more.

fit & healthy

Both the ingredients and methods of food preparation in Morocco are conducive to healthy eating. Staples here comprise a varied diet, and freshness is a priority to Moroccan cooks. As long as you follow the basic rules of hygiene and nutrition, you can get on with the business of culinary pleasure.

Don't plan on hitting the ground running, especially if you're on a long trip. It's worth allowing yourself time to adjust physically and mentally to your new environment and lifestyle, especially in the first week. Factor in some time to take a breather, recover from jet lag and catch up on sleep.

Morocco is relatively free of unhealthy bugs, and most Moroccans are assiduous when it comes to making sure food is fresh and healthy. The nature of Moroccan cooking – generally long and slow – tends to stop bugs from flourishing. However, as refrigeration is confined to the urban centres, being careful about how, what and where you eat is important. If you're eating at a restaurant, you're unlikely to be in danger unless it's a question of sheer bad luck (which can happen anywhere). Beware of fly-blown cafes, and prepared food that looks as if it has been displayed for ages in the sun.

In many months spent travelling through Morocco, the only grief we suffered in terms of hygiene was a couple of medium-to-bad stomach upsets probably due to eating raw salads washed in water of dubious quality. Eating cooked foods and cooked salads is a more sensible idea.

Hygiene

Many diseases associated with warm countries are actually diseases of poor hygiene. So it's worth reminding yourself to wash your hands before you eat (there's usually a basin or jug for this in most restaurants) and always after using the toilet. Short fingernails are easier to keep clean than long ones.

Water

Water in Morocco is inconsistent in quality. It is reputedly safe to drink unless marked otherwise. However, water is a notorious carrier of bugs in any region of the world, so drinking bottled water is safer. Certainly in the mountainous regions of Morocco, bottled water is advised. Given its wide availability and negligible price, it is wise to stick to bottled water where possible. If bottled water is unavailable then it's advisable to boil any water you find. Major hotels insist that their water is absolutely fine for drinking, although we can report that the taste test often leaves an unpleasant tang. Water used to make hot coffee or tea is of course boiled, rendering it safe to drink.

If you are unsure about the water, don't risk the ice.

Fluid Balance

Plain water, lots of it, is the best preventative and remedy for dehydration. Always carry a supply of drinking water with you and remind yourself to sip from it regularly while you're out.

Use how much urine you're passing as a rough guide to whether you're getting dehydrated. Small amounts of dark urine suggest you need to increase your fluid intake.

Eating the Right Stuff

Eating well should be fun, but it's also about making sure you get enough of the right nutrients to enable you to function at your best, mentally and physically. When you're travelling, your diet will be different from normal; in addition, a different lifestyle, stress and new activities may mean your nutritional requirements are increased.

With the help of this book you'll be able to identify available foods for a diverse and nutritious diet. But when you eat can be as important as what you eat. If you're on the move, be careful not to miss meals as this will make you more easily fatigued and vulnerable to illness.

THE BASICS

Everybody needs six basics for life: water, carbohydrates, protein, fat, vitamins and minerals. Foods aren't a pure source of just one type of nutrient, they contain various elements in different quantities, so the best way to make sure you get enough of the right elements is to eat a varied diet.

As a guide, you need to eat a variety of foods from each of five core groups:

- bread, other cereals – eat lots of these, they provide carbohydrate, fibre, some calcium and iron, and B vitamins
- fruit & vegetables – eat lots of these, they give you vitamin C, carotenes (vitamin A), folate, fibre and some carbohydrate
- milk and dairy products – eat moderate amounts for calcium, zinc, protein, vitamin B12, vitamin B2, vitamin A and vitamin D
- meat, fish, nuts, beans – these provide iron, protein, B vitamins (especially B12; meat only), zinc and magnesium; eat in moderation
- fat and sugary foods (butter, oil, margarine, cakes, biscuits, sweets, etc) – eat sparingly from this group, which mainly provides fat, including essential fatty acids, some vitamins and salt

Bear in mind that if you're already sick, your requirements change and you may need to increase the amounts of some food groups to increase your intake of protein, vitamins and minerals, for example.

Fading Away?

Losing weight when you're travelling is pretty common. There are lots of reasons for this, including getting sick, having a change in diet and perhaps being more active. You may have a bit of padding to spare, but keep an eye on how much weight you're losing and don't allow yourself to shed too much. If you do shed too much weight too quickly, you may put yourself at risk of illness, as well as being drained of your energy.

If you've just turned vegetarian – or don't trust the meat here – be aware that your body takes a bit of time to adjust to getting some nutrients from plant sources, so it's worth taking a bit of care with your diet. Getting enough protein isn't generally a problem, especially if you eat dairy products or eggs. Note that proteins from plant sources often lack one or more amino acids (the building blocks of protein). Most traditionally vegetarian diets have dealt with this by basing meals around a combination of protein sources so that deficiencies are complemented. Examples of combinations include: pulses and rice, pulses and cereal, and nuts and cereal.

Because iron from plant sources is less well absorbed than iron from meat, iron-deficiency anaemia is a risk if you aren't careful, especially in menstruating women. Another vitamin you might not get enough of is vitamin B12 as it's only derived from animal sources. If you cut out all animal foods from your diet, you'll need to take a supplement to make up for this.

Good plant sources of nutrients include:

protein	pulses, bread, rice, noodles, seeds, potatoes
calcium	seeds, green leafy vegetables, nuts, bread, dried fruit
iron	pulses, green vegetables, dried fruits, nuts; absorption of iron is increased by consuming a source of vitamin C at the same time (fruit, fruit juice or vegetables); tea, coffee, and phytate and oxalates from plants will reduce the absorption of iron

Diarrhoea

Diarrhoea can be caused by an ingested bug. Often, slight diarrhoea is your body's response to new food and a different environment, and will settle down after a few days, merely requiring a few extra bathroom stops. However, a serious dose can prevent you from enjoying your stay or worse, make you seriously ill.

First rule to avoid diarrhoea is to avoid untreated water – stick to the bottled water and if possible, check where raw salads have been washed. If you're really a stickler, you'll also brush your teeth using bottled water when the water supply seems uncertain.

Essaouira

If you are caught with a mild dose of diarrhoea, then the over-the-counter medications, Lomotil and Imodium, are found in most pharmacies. These provide relief but do not provide a cure. Make sure you replace lost fluids with as much water as possible. Mint tea, with its combination of stomach-calming mint and sugar, is a very good option. Moroccans advise taking a spoonful of cumin and washing it down with plenty of water. Flat lemonade or soft drink are other helpful fluids.

While suffering from diarrhoea, avoid the richer Moroccan foods. Stick to bread and simple grills or cooked salads. Excessive butter and oil are best avoided. If diarrhoea includes blood and mucus (Lomotil and Iomodium should be avoided in this case), persists for more than about five days, or worsens, you should consult a doctor as soon as possible – it may be an indication that you're suffering from something serious.

Recovering from diarrhoea should involve lots of rehydration. Buy a gastrolyte preparation from the local pharmacy to help your system return to normal. While most pharmacies carry this sort of thing, it may be wise to pack some sachets before you go – in that way, if you find yourself in a remoter part of the country you will have it with you.

What to Eat

It's easy to get hung up about what, if anything, to eat when you have diarrhoea. But relax, use your common sense and try to tune in to what your body is telling you – if you feel like eating, go ahead, especially starchy foods known to promote salt and water absorption. If you don't feel like eating, don't force yourself to. Unless you're really roughing it, you're going to be basically well nourished and well able to withstand a couple of days with little or no food. It may make you feel a bit wobbly, so make sure you add a bit of sugar or honey to your drinks to keep your energy levels up.

Your overworked stomach will appreciate small amounts of food at regular intervals rather than great big meals, and this may help make you feel less nauseated too. You may find that eating brings on cramps and you have to dash to the toilet. We all

Food on the Runs

When you have diarrhoea, it's good to eat:

- plain rice
- plain noodles
- dry biscuits, salty or not too sweet

plain couscous, steamed and without butter and oil

If possible, it's best to avoid:

- fruit & vegetables, except bananas
- dairy products, including yoghurt
- spicy foods
- greasy foods

have a natural reflex whereby eating increases the activity of the gut, but this can get exaggerated in a diarrhoeal illness. It doesn't make you a great dinner companion, but you'll probably find that once you've answered the call of nature you can return to finish your meal! (But remember to wash your hands very thoroughly…)

Contrary to the spirit of this book, you should stick to a more limited diet while you have diarrhoea and as you recover. You should also go easy on fibre providers like fruit, vegetables and nuts. Bananas are good as they tend to stop you up, and are a source of potassium and glucose. As the diarrhoea clears up and you start to get your appetite back, add in more foods gradually until you're back to normal and can resume your culinary escapade.

Indigestion

A change in diet, stress, anxiety and spicy foods can all make 'indigestion' (burning pains in your upper abdomen) and heartburn (burning in your gullet, often with an acid taste in your mouth) more likely when you're travelling. The discomfort is often worse when you're hungry or just after meals. Smoking and alcohol exacerbate it.

Simple measures you could try are to eat small, regular meals – don't eat a huge meal just before you go to bed and try to avoid spicy hot foods. Milk and yoghurt can be soothing, as can eating plain, starchy foods. Consider trying antacids (there are many products available without prescription), although stomach acid has a protective effect against infective agents, so taking antacids may make you more vulnerable to gut infections.

Children

Children may find that the more heavily spiced Moroccan dishes are not to their taste, although there is no real reason why any Moroccan food should be deliberately avoided by children. Moroccans do not give children certain delicacies before they reach puberty – these are brains, testicles, tripe and noses. Travelling parents may want to follow the locals' lead, here.

Allergies

Allergies to ingredients such as nuts are quite easy to manage in Morocco. Nuts are usually added as a decorative and textural element at the end of the cooking process and so can be simply removed. When you order, you should request that they are not included. If you are allergic to nuts, avoid all pastries – apart from pancakes – because crushed almonds are most often used in the fillings.

Shellfish is unlikely to be included in a dish unless specified.

Diabetics

Diabetics should be wary of the high sugar content of mint tea. Although animal fat is not often used in Moroccan cooking, it can be quite rich in oil.

Fat & Cholesterol

While fat content is quite high in some Moroccan dishes, it is usually through the addition of oil rather than animal fat, as lean meat is favoured in tajines and couscous. Moroccans traditionally like to use quite a lot of oil and a generous dose of **smen** (aged butter), although these days there is a definite preference for recipes adapted with less of these weighty ingredients – the Moroccans call it 'modern' cooking. Salads are generally made with olive oil, and canola or other types of vegetable oils are used in tajines and couscous. Moroccan pastries and pancakes are relatively high in calories.

Recommended Reading

La Cuisine Marocaine, **Latifa Benanni-Smires,** Morocco, 1997

A Short History of Africa, **Oliver and Fage,** Penguin, 1977

The Moroccan Cookbook, **Irene F Day,** Quick Fox, 1975

Good Food from Morocco, **Paula Wolfert,** John Murray, 1989

Come With Me to the Kasbah, A Cook's Tour of Morocco, **Kitty Morse,** Morocco, 1989

Moorish Food, **Sarah Woodward,** Kylie Cathie Limited, 1998

Taste of Morocco, **Robert Carrier,** Arrow Books, 1987

Street Cafe Morocco, **Anissa Helou,** Conran Octopus, 1988

Food in History, **Reay Tannahill,** Penguin, 1988

A New Book of Middle Eastern Food, **Claudia Roden,** Penguin, 1986

Fés vu par sa Cuisine, **Mme Guinaudeau,** Morocco, 1958

Fudalat al-Khiwan, **Ibn Razin Tujubi,** Morocco, 1997

Morocco, **Lonely Planet,** Australia, 1998

Photo Credits

Catherine Hanger Front cover, p1, p9 top left & right, bottom left, p11, p16, p23, p26, p27, p31, p34, p35, p40, p41, p47, p51, p54, p55, 58, p62, p67 top right, bottom left & right, p68, p75, p79, p81 top left, bottom left & right, p82, p85, p 86, p90, p95, p97 top right, bottom left & right, p107 top left, bottom left & right, p109, p115 top left & right, bottom right, p123, p126, p127 top, p128, p131, p133, p134, p136, p138, p140, p144, p145, p147, p149 top left & right, bottom left, p151, p153, p155 top & bottom left.

Greg Elms p5, p8, p29, p38, p39, p43, p57, p63, p64, p65, p113 middle right, p115 bottom left, p149 bottom left.

Veronica Garbutt p18, p60, p78, p111, p113 top right, p127 bottom, p155.

Mark Daffey p14, p104, p116, 146.

Nick Ray p67 top left, p72, p113 bottom left.

Christine Osborne p77, p97 top left, back cover.

Oliver Ciredini p113 middle left, p150, p158.

Damien Simons p9 bottom right, p52.

Adam McCrow p17, p92.

Oliver Strewe p28, p113 bottom right.

Jerry Alexander p37.

Alan Benson p76.

Simon Bracken p42.

Frances Linzee Gordon p101.

Patrick Syder p44.

eat your words

language guide

PRONUNCIATION

Several Moroccan Arabic sounds will be new to the native English speaker and difficult at first to pronounce so we have simplified the transliteration as much as possible. Take comfort in the fact that perfect pronunciation isn't necessary for you to be understood and that Moroccans are patient and always willing to help.

Vowels

Short Vowels

a as the 'a' in 'at'
e as the 'a' in 'about'
i as the 'i' in 'hit'
u as the 'oo' in 'book'

Long Vowels

ā as the 'a' in 'father'
ī as the 'ee' in 'see'
ō as the 'oa' in 'boat'
ū as the 'oo' in 'boot'

Consonants

Many Moroccan Arabic consonants are similar to English, but there are some you should note.

g as the 'g' in 'go' not as the 'g' in 'gentle'
gh a guttural 'r' approximated by gargling gently. Similar to the French 'r'.
h similar to the English 'h' but pronounced deep in the throat with a loud raspy whisper
kh like the 'kh' in German 'Bach'
H a strongly whispered 'h' almost like a sigh of relief
q like the 'k' in 'king' but pronounced further back in the throat
zh as the 's' in 'pleasure'
' a glottal stop, like the sound heard between the vowels in 'uh-oh'
c a tricky sound that may be approximated by saying the 'a' in fat with the tongue against the bottom of the mouth and from as deep in the throat as possible

Emphatic Consonants

ḍ ṣ ṭ emphatic consonants are pronounced with more tension in the mouth and throat and with the back of the tongue raised toward the roof of the mouth, like when prolonging the 'l' sound in 'pull'.

USEFUL PHRASES

Eating Out

restaurant
  risṭura/maṭᶜam — ريسطورا\مطعم

cheap restaurant
  maṭᶜam rkhīṣ — مطعم رخيص
  risṭura rkhīṣa — ريسطورا رخيصة

Do you speak English?
  kataᶜraf nnagliza? — كاتعرف النكليزية
  wāsh katādar bnnagliza? — واش كتهدر بالنكليزية

Table for ..., please.
  ṭabla dyāl ... ᶜafāk — طبلة ديال ... عفاك

Can I pay by credit card?
  wash nkder nkhelleṣ — واش نقدر نخلص
  bel kārt kreḍī? — باكرت كريدي؟

Do you have a highchair for the baby?
  ᶜandak shi kursi ᶜāli — عانداك شي كرسي
  dyāl ddrāri? — عالي ديال الدراري

Just Try It!

What's that?
  shnu hāda? — شنو هذا

What's the speciality of this region?
  shnu lmākla lli khāṣṣaa — شنو الماكلة اللي خاصّة
  bhād nnāнiyya/lblād? — بهاد الناحية\بهاد البلاد

What's the speciality here?
  shnu lmākla dyālkum hnā? — شنو الماكلة ديالكوم هنا

What do you recommend?
  shnu ᶜandkum ldīd/zwīn? — شنو عندكم لديد\زوين
  shnu tanṣānī nākul? — شنو تنصحني ناكل

What are they eating?
  āsh tayāklā? — آش تياكلو

I'll try what she's having.
  gha nzharrab shnu kātakul hiyya — غانجرب شنو كاتكل هي

The Menu

Can I see the menu please?
naqdar naᶜraf lmākla lli ᶜandkum? نقدر نعرف الماكلة للي عندكم
yamkan lī nshuf يمكن لي نشوف
lmuni llā ykhallīk? الموني آلله يخليك

Do you have a menu in English?
wāsh ᶜandkum llista dyāl واش عاندكم الليستا
lmākla bnnagliza? ديال الماكلة بالنكليزة
wāsh ᶜandkum lmuni bnnagliza? واش عاندكم الموني بالنكليزة

What are today's specials?
shnu mṭṭayybīn lyūm? شنو مطيبين ليوم

I'd like the set lunch, please.
bghīt āna ntkallaf bl ghda, بغيت أنا نتكلف
llā ykhallik بالغداء الله يخليك

What does it include?
shnu fīh? شنو فيه

Is service included in the bill?
wāsh ssarbīs dkāhil flaHsā? واش السربيس داخل فالحساب

Does it come with salad?
ghādi tzhi mᶜāh shshlāḍa? غادي تجي معه الشلادة

What's the soup of the day?
shnu hiyya ṣṣubba dyāl lyūm? شنو هيا الصّوبا ديال ليوم

Throughout the Meal

What's in this dish?
āshnu fhād lmākla? آشنو فهاد الماكلة

Not too spicy please.
mā tkūnsh Hārra ᶜafāk ماتكونش حارة عفاك

Is that dish spicy?
wāsh hād lmākla Hārra? واش هاذ الماكلة حارة

It's not hot.
mā skhunāsh (opposed to cold) ماسخوناش
mā Hārrash (opposed to mild) ماحرّاش

I didn't order this.
ṭlabtsh hād shshi ما طلبتش هاذ الشي

I'd like ...	bghīt ...	بغيت ...
Please bring me ...	llā ykhallīk zhīb lī ...	الله يخليك جيبلي ...
some water	shwiyya dyāl lmā	شويا ديال الما
some wine	shwiyya dyāl shshrāb	شويا ديال الشراب
some salt	shwiyya dyāl lmalнa	شويا ديال الملحا
some pepper	shwiyya dyāl libzār	شويا ديال لبزار
some bread	shwiyya dyāl lkhūbz	شويا ديال الخبز
an ashtray	ṣṣāndriyyi/	الصاندريي\
	ḍḍaffaya	الضفّايا
a glass	kās	كاس
a cup	ṭṭāsa	الطّاسة
a fork	furshiṭa/shūka	فورشيطة\شوكة
a knife	sakkīn	سكين
a spoon	mᶜalqa	معلقة
a plate	ṭabsīl/ghtār	طابسيل\غطار
a teaspoon	mᶜalqa sghīra	صغيرة معلقة
a toothpick	lkhshība dyāl ssnān	الخشيبة ديال السنان
	bashnikha	بشنيخة
a napkin	mandīl	منديل
more wine	zīdni shshrāb	زيدني الشّراب

This food is ...	hād lmākla ...	هاذ الماكلا ...
brilliant	mazyāna/bnīna	مزيانا\بنينا
burnt	maнrūqa	محروقا
cold	bārdā	باردا
stale	bāslā	باسلا
spoiled	khāyba	خايبا
undercooked	mā ṭaybāsh mazyān	ما طايباش مزيان

I'd like something to drink.
bghīt shi нāzha nashrubha — بغيت شي حاجة نشربها

Can I have a (beer) please?
bghīt shi (birra) ᶜafāk — بغيت شي [بيرّا] عفاك

Can you please bring me ...?
taqdar ᶜafāk tzh?bli ... — تقدر عفاك تجيبلي ...

Thank you, that was delicious.
llā yakhlaf, hād shshi bnīn/ldīd — هادشي بنين\لديد,الله يخلف

Please pass on our compliments to the chef.
shkūr shshāf man
ᶜandi llā ykhallīk
qul lshshāf tbārk llā ᶜlīh
شكُر الشاّف من
عنديالله يخلّيكقول
للشّاف تبارك الله عليه

The bill, please.
laHsāb, ᶜafāk
عافاك,الحساب

You May Hear

Anything else?
shī Hāzha ’ukhra?
شي حاجة أخرى

Family Meals

You’re a great cook!
llāh ya ᶜtik ṣṣaHa
tbārk llāh ᶜlīk
الله يعطيك الصحة
تبارك الله عليك

This is brilliant!
had shshi ldīd bazzīf
had shshi zwīn bazzāf
هاذ الشي لذيذ بزّاف
هاد الشّي زْوين بزاّف

Do you have the recipe for this?
kīfāsh kaṭṭayybu hād lmākla
كيفاش كتطيبو هاذ الماكلة

Is this a family recipe?
wāsh hāda ṭyāb dyāl
واش هذا طياب ديال ملولين الدار

Are the ingredients local?
hād shshi bāsh
kaṭṭayybuh kullu muzhud?
هاد الشي باش
كتطيبوه كلو موجود

What are the ingredients?
wāsh hād lqwām muzhud?
واشْ هاد لْقْوامْ موجود

I’ve never had a meal like this before.
maᶜammri maklīt shi
mākla bHāl hādi
ما عمّري ما كليت
شي ماكلة بحال هاذي

Could you pass the (salt) please?
yamkan līk taᶜtini
(lmalHa) lla ykhallik?
taqdar taᶜtini (lmalHa) ᶜafak?
يمكن لك تعطيني
[لْمْلْحَة] الله يخلّيك؟
تْقْدْرْ تْعْطيني [لْمْلْحَة] عْفاك ؟

Thanks very much for the meal.
tanshakrak bazzāf ᶜal lmākla
تنشكرك بزّاف على الماكلة

I really appreciate it.
hād shshi ᶜzhabnī bazzāf — هاد الشي عجبني بزاّف
bāraka llāhu fīk — بارك الله فيك

Vegetarian & Special Meals

I'm a vegetarian.
makanakūlsh llнam — ما كنكولش اللحم

I'm a vegan, I don't eat meat or dairy products.
makanakul la llнam la нatta нazha lli fīha lнlīb — ما كانكل لا اللحم لا حتى حاجة اللي فيها الحليب

Do you have any vegetarian dishes?
wāsh ᶜandkum shi mākla mā fihāsh llнam? — واش عنكم شي ماكلة ما فيهاش اللحم

Can you recommend a vegetarian dish, please?
ᶜandkum shi mākla blā lнam yamkallik tanṣaнni bīha? — عندكم شي ماكلة بلا لحم يمكّن لك تنصحني بها

Does this dish have meat?
wāsh hād ṭṭyāb fīh llнam? — واش هاذ الطياب فيه اللحم

Can I get this without the meat?
yamkalli nākhud hāda blā lнam? — يمكللي ناخذ هذا بلا لحم

Does it contain eggs/dairy products?
wāsh fīh lbīḍ/mawādd lнlīb? — واش فيه البيض\مواد الحليب

I'm allergic to (peanuts).
mākanakulsh/kayḍarrnī (kāwkāw) — ما كانكلش\كايضرّني [كاوكاو]

I don't eat ...	mākanakuls ...	ماكانكلش ...
meat	llнam	اللحم
chicken	ddzhāzh	الدجاج
fish	lнūt	الحوت
pork	lнallūf	الحلّوف

Is it ...-free?	wāsh blā ...	واش ...؟
wheat	zraᶜ	بلا زرع
salt	malнa	بلا ملحة
sugar	sukkar	بلا سكّر
yeast	khmīhra	بلا خميرة

At the Market

Where's the nearest (market)?
fayn zha 'aqrab (mārshī)? — فاين جا أقرب [مارشي]

How much?
bshHāl? — بشحال

Can I have a ...	bghīt ...	بغيت ...
	ᶜṭīni ...	عطيني ...
bottle	qarᶜa	قرعة
box	rbīᶜa/ṣanduq	ربيعة\صندوق
can	Hukk	حك
packet	bakiyya	بكية
sachet/bag	khansha	خنشة
tin of ...	Hukk dyāl ...	حكّ ديال ...

Will this keep in the fridge?
yamkan līha tabqa fittallazha? — يمكن ليها تبقا فالتلاّجا

How much is
(a kilo of cheese)?
bshHāl (kīlu dyāl lfrūmāzh)? — بشحال [كيلو ديال لفرماج]

Do you have anything cheaper?
ᶜandak shi Hazha — عندك شي حاجة
rkhaṣ man hādshi? — رخص من هادشي

Is this the best you have?
wāsh hād shshi 'aHsan mā ᶜandak? — واش هادشي أحسان ما عندك
wāsh hād shshi huwwa rās ssuq? — واش هادشي هو راس السوق

What's the local speciality?
shnū kayāklu f hād lblād? — شنو كاياكلو في هاد البلاد

Give me (half) a kilo, please.
ᶜṭīni (nuṣṣ) kīlu, ᶜafāk — عفاك,عطيني [نص] كيلو

I'd like (six slices of ham).
bghīt (stta ṭranshiyyāt — بغيت [ستّا طرانشيّات
dyāl zhzhambun) — ديال الجّامبون]

Can I taste it?
naqdar ndūq? — نقدر ندوق

Where can I find the (sugar)?
fāyn naqdar nalqa (ssukār)? — فاين نقدر نلقا [السكار]

I'd like some ...	bghīt shwiyya dyāl ...	بغيت شويا ديال ...
biscuits	bīskwi/bashkītū	بيسكوي\يشكيطو
bread	lkhubz	الخبز
butter	zzabda	الزبدة
cheese	lfrumāzh	لفرماج
	zhzhban	الجبن
chocolate	shshuklāṭ	الشّكلاط
eggs	lbīḍ	البيض
flour	ṭṭHīn	الطحين
frozen foods	mākla kunzhli/	ماكلا كونجلي\
	mtallzha	متلّجا
fruit & vegetables	lfawākih w lkhuḍra	الفواكه والخضرا
ham	zhzhābūn	الجّامبون
honey	laᶜsal	العسل
jam	lkūnfitīr	الكونفيتير
margarine	lmārgarīn	الماركارين
marmalade	lkūnfitīr	الكونفيتير
milk	lHlīb	الحليب
olive oil	zīt zzitūn	زيت الزيتون
	zīt lᶜud	زيت العود
	zzīt lbaldiyya	الزيت البلدية
sunflower oil	zīt nawwart shshams	زيت نوّارة الشمس
	zzīt rrumiyya	الزيت الرومية
pepper	libzār	ليبزار
salt	lmalHa	الملحا
sugar	ssukār	السكار
yoghurt	dānūn	دانون
... olives	zzitūn ...	الزيتون ...
black	lkhal	لكحل
green	lkhdar	لخضر
stuffed	mᶜammar	معمّر

At the Bar

Shall we go for a drink?
nmshīw nsharbū shī Hāzha? — نمشيو نشربو شي حاجة

I'll buy you a drink.
ghādi nashrī līk shī mashrūb — غادي نشريلك شي مشروب
ghādi nkhallas ᶜlīk shī Hāzha — غادي نخلّص عليك شي حاجة

Thanks, but I don't feel like it.
shūkran, walākin mā fiyya mā nashrūb — ولكن ما فيّ ما نشرب,شكرا

I don't drink (alcohol).
mā kanashrūbsh (shshrāb) — ما كنشربش [الشّراب]

What would you like?
shnū bghītī — شنو بغيتي

It's on me.
'ana lli ghādī nkhallaṣ — أنا اللي غادي نخلّص

You can get the next one.
khallaṣ nta nnūba zhzhāyya — خلّص أنت النوبة الجّايّة

OK.	wākhkha	واخّا
I'm next.	'ana mnbaᶜd	أنا من بعد
Excuse me.	smāнli	سماحلي
Cheers!	bṣaннatkum	بصحّتكم

I'll have (a) ...	bghīt/ᶜtīni ...	بغيت\عطيني ...
beer	birra	بيرا
liqueur	likūr	ليكور
brandy	brāndī	براندي
champagne	shampanya	شامبانيا
cocktail	kūktīl	كوكتيل
cider	ssidr	السيدر
rum	rrūm	الرّوم
whisky	lwīskī	الويسكي
glass of wine	kās dyāl shshrāb	كاس ديال الشّراب
bottle of wine	qarᶜa dyāl shshrāb	قرعا ديال الشّراب
(two) glasses	(zhuzh) dyāl lkīsān	[زوز] ديال الكيسان

Can I have ice, please.
bghīt ttalzh, ᶜafāk — عفاك,بغيت التلج

No ice.
blah talzh — بلا تلج

Same again, please.
nafs shshi, llā ykhallīk — الله يخليك,نفس الشي

Is food available here?
wāsh ᶜandkūm lmākla hnā? — واش عندكم الماكلة هنا

Where's the toilet?
fāyn lmirнāḍ ᶜafāk? — فاين المرحاض عفاك
fāyn ṭṭwālīṭ llā ykhallīk? — فاين الطواليط الله يخلّيك

This is hitting the spot.
zhāt fblāṣthā — جات فبلاصتها.

I'm a bit tired, I'd better get home.
'ana shwiyya ta^cbān,
min l'āsan namshi lddār — من الأحسن نمشي لدّار
أنا شويّا تعبان,

I'm feeling drunk.
kānнass brāsi skart — كانحسّ براسي سكرت

I feel ill.
kanнass brāsi māshi hūwa hadāk — كانحسّ براسي ماشي هو هاداك

Wine

May I see the wine list, please?
nshūf shnū ᶜandkum
f shshrāb, ᶜafāk — نشوف شنو عندكم
في الشراب، عفاك

Can you recommend a good local wine?
ᶜandkūm shi shrāb
mgharbi mzyān? — عندكم شي شراب
مغربي مزيان

May I taste it?
naqdar ndūqu? — نقدر ندوقو

Which wine would you
recommend with this dish?
'āsh mn shrāb ywālm hād lmākla? — آش من شراب يوالم هاد الماكلة

I'd like a glass/ bottle of ... wine.	bghīt kās/qarᶜa dyāl ... shshrāb	بغيت كاس\قرعة ديال ... الشراب
red	нmar/rūzh	حمر\روج
white	byaḍ/blān	بيض\بلان
rose	rūzī	روزي

This is brilliant!
hād shshi zwīn/ᶜazhīb — هادشي زوين\عجيب

This wine has a nice/bad taste.
hād shshrāb madāqu zwīn/khāyab — هاد الشراب مداقو زوين\خايب

This wine has a nice/bad colour.
hād shshrāb lūnū zwīn/khāyab — هاد الشراب لونو زوين\خايب

This wine is corked.
hād shshrāb fīh ṭībt lbūshūn — هاد الشراب فيه طيبة البوشون

The transliteration used in this dictionary contains symbols not found in the English alphabet (refer to the Pronunciation section for explanation).

We have included the symbols in this Eat Your Words section for accuracy but have left them out of the main text for ease of use.

A

absinth	shshība	الشيبة
alcoholic sodas	shshrāb	الشراب
ale	bīrra	بيرة
almonds	llūz	اللوز
anchovy	lanshwa/lshṭūn	لانشوا\الشطون
angelica	mᶜadnūs	معدنوس
anise	nnāfaᶜ	النافع
aperitif	lqaṭᶜa/lāpiritif	لقطعا\لابيتيف
appetiser	lanṭri/shlāḍa	لنطري\شلاظا
apples	ttuffaH	التفاح
apricot	lbarqūq/mashmāsh	البرقوق
artichoke	lqūq	القوق
asparagus	lizasperzh/ssakkūm	ليزاسبيرج\السكوم
aubergine	lbdanzhāl	البادنجال
avocado	lāvukā	الافوكا

B

baby corn	ddrā ṣṣghīra	الدّرا الصّغيرا
bacon	lHam l Hallūf	لحم الحلّوف
bake	khbaz/ṭraH	خبز\طرح
baking soda	lkhmīra	الخميرا
banana	banāna/lmūz	بانانا\الموز
barbeque	shshwā	الشوا
barbeque grill	lmazhmar	المجمر
barley	balbūla/shshᶜīr	الشعير\البلبولا
basmati rice	rrūzz rrūmi	الروز الرّومي
bass	shshābal	الشابل
batter	lᶜzhīna	العجينا
bay leaves	wrāq sidna mūsa/laurier	وراق سيدنا موسى\اللوريي

bean	lūbya	لوبيا
beef	lbaqri	البقري
beer	lbīrra	البيرا
beetroot	lbārba	الباربا
berries	ttūt	التوت
bill	lHsāb/lādition	الحساب\الاديسيون
bird's eye chilli	ṣṣūdaniyya ṣṣghīra	السودانيّا الصغيرا
biscuits	beshkīṭu/biskwī	بشكيطو\بيسكوي
bitter lemon	llīmun lmer/ lmṣayyar	اللّيمون المرّ\ المصيّر
bitters	ttHāmaḍ	التحامض
black(-eyed) bean	fūl gnāwa	فول چناوا
black olive	zītūn kHal	زيتون كحل
blackberry	tūt rrūmi	التوت الرومي
blender	miksūr/ṭaHHana	ميكسور\طحّانا
blueberry	tūt l'arḍ	توت الأرض
to boil	ghalla	غلّا
bok choy	lkrūm ṣṣghīr	الكروم الصّغير
bottle/can opener	Hallala	حلالة
bowl	zlāfa/zhabbaniya	زلافا\جبّانيّا
brain	mukhkh	مخ
braise	shwī	شوي
bran	nnakhāla	النخّالا
brandy	brāndi	براندي
bread	khubz/khobz	خبز
breakfast	fṭūr	فطور
breast	ṣṣder	الصدر
brisket	lHam ḍḍalᶜa	لحم الضلعا
broad bean	lūbya lkbīra	لوبيا الكبيرا
broccoli	brokoli	بروكولي
broth	lmerqa/laṣūṣ	لمرقا\الاصوص
brown lentil	lᶜadess	العدس
brown rice	rrūzz rrūmi	الروز الرّومي
brown sauce	lmerqa lmqallya	المرقة المقلّيا
brussels sprouts	lishū d bruksīl	ليشو د بروكسيل
burghul	ttshīsha	التشيشة
butter	zzebda	الزبدا
buttermilk	llben	اللبن
butternut squash	qarᶜa takhrifīn	چرعا تاخيفين

C

cabbage	lkrūm	لكروم
cakes	Halwa/ddwāz datāy	حلوى/الدّواز د آتاي
candy	fanīd/lHalwa	فنيد\ الحلوى
cantaloupe	battīkh/sswihla/ lkanṭalū	بتي\السويهلة\و الكانطالخ
capers	kubbār	كبّار
caramel	kāramil	كراميل
caraway seed	karwiyya	كرويا
cardoon	qannariyya/kharshūf	قنّريّا\خرشوف
cashew	kāwkāw rrūmi	كاوكاو الرّومي
cauliflower	shūflūr	شيفلور
caviar	kāvyār	كافيار
cayenne	ṣṣūdaniyya	السودانيا
celery	sīlrī	سيلري
cereal	ssīryāl	السيريال
champagne	shampanya	شامبانيا
cheese	frumazh/zhben	فرماج\جبن
blue	lblū	البلو
cottage	lbaldi/klīla	البلدي\كليلة
cream	dlākrīm	دلاكريم
goat's	dlma^{c}za	دالمعزة
chef	shshāf	الشاف
cheque	lHsāb/lādition	الحساب\لاديسيون
cherries	Habb lmlūk	حبّ الملوك
cherry tomatoes	maṭisha sghīra	مطيشا صغيرا
chestnut	qesṭāl	قسطال
chicken	dzhāzh	دجاج
chickpeas	Hammus	حمص
chicory	shshīkurī	الشيكوري
chilli	lHrūr	الحرور
chinese cabbage	lkrūm ṣṣghīr	الكروم الصغير
chips	baṭaṭa maqliyya/ tships	بطاطا مقليّ\ تشيبسا
chives	lbūrru	البورّو
chocolate	shklāṭ	شكلاط
chopping board	lkhashba dttaqtā^{c}	الخشبة د التقطاع
chops	ḍḍal^{c}a	الضّلعة
chorizo	ṣṣuṣīṣ	الصوصيص

chowder	ṣṣūbba d lHūt	الصّوبّا د الحوت
cinnamon	qarfa	قرفة
citrus	lHawamiḍ	الحوامض
cloves	qrunfal	قرنفل
cocktail	kuktīl	كوكتيل
coconut	lkūkū	الكوكو
cod	lāmurī	الاموري
coffee	lqahwa	القهوة
coffee grinder	ṭaHHana dl qahwa	طحّانا د القهوا
coffee machine	mākina dl qahwa	ماكنا د القهوا
coke	kuka kula	كوكاكولا
condiments	l^{c}atriyya	العطرية
cookies	bshkīṭu	بشكيطو
coriander	qeṣbūr	قصبور
corn	ddrā	الدّرا
cornflakes	kurn fliks	كورن فليكس
cornmeal	ṭHin d ddrā/ Halwa d ddrā	طحين الدّرا\ حلوا د الدّرا
courgette	qar^{c}a	لچرعا
couscous	seksū	سكسو
crab	lkrab	الكراب
cracked wheat	zzra^{c} mharmaṣh	الزّرع مهرمش
cranberry	tūt l'arḍ	توت الأرض
cream	lakrīm	لاكريم
croissant	krwaṣṣa	كرواصّا
cucumber	lkhyār	الخيار
cumin	kammūn	كمون
cup	ṭṭaṣa	الطاسا
currant	nnbaq	النبق
curry	lkuri	الكوري
curry powder	lkuri madqūq	الكوري مدقوق
cutlets	lkuṭlīṭ	الكوتليت

D

date/dates	tamra/ttmer	تمرة\التمر
deep-fry	qli	قلي
dessert	ddissīr	الديسير
dessert spoon	m^{c}alqa d ddissīr	معلقا د الدّيسير
dewberry	tūt l'arḍ	توت الأرض
dinner	l^{c}sha	العشا

dried fruit	fākya yābsa	فاكيا يابسا
drinks	mashrūbāt	مشروبات
duck	lbaṭṭa	البطه

E

eel	ṣṣamta	الصّمطا
eggplant	lbdanzhāl	البادنجال
eggs	lbīḍ	البيض
endive	lizandīv	الليزنديف
entree	lanṭri	لانطري

F

feet	hergma	هرجمة
fennel	lfunūy	الفونوى
fennel seed	zarriᶜt lfunūy	زريعة آلفونوي
fig	kermūṣ	كرموص
fillet	lfīli	لفيلي
fish	Hūt	حوت
flank	būṣwīṭ	بوسويط
flavour	madāq	مداق
flour	tHīn	طحين
food processor	robo d lkuzina	روبو د الكوزينا
fork	shūka/fursheṭa	شوكا\فورشيطا
frankfurter	ṣṣuṣīṣ	الصوصيص
fresh juice	ᶜaṣīr trī	عصير طري
frog	zhrāna	جرانا
fruit	fåkya	فاكية
fruit cake	Halwa blfākya	حلوآ بالفاكيا
fruit juice	ᶜaṣīr lfākya	عصير الفاكيا
fruit punch	ᶜaṣīr mkhallaṭ	عصير مخلّط
fry	qli	قلي
frying pan	maqla	مقلا

G

garlic	thūm	ثوم
garlic press	ṭaHHāna dthūm	طحّانا دالثوم
gherkin	kurnishon	كورنيشون
ginger	skīn zhbīr	سكينجبير

goose	lwezz	الوزّ
gooseberry	ttūt rrūmi	التوت الرّومي
grapefruit	pamplumūs	لبامبلوموس
grapes	l^{c}inab	العنب
to grate	Hakk	حك
grater	mHekka	محكا
gravy	marqa	مرقا
grease	shaHma	شحما
green lentil	l^{c}adess lkhaḍra	العدس الخضرا
green olive	zzītūn lkhḍar	الزيتون الخضر
grill	shwi	شوي

H

ham	zhambūn	جامبون
hamburger	hamburger	هامبورچر
hare	larnab	لرنب
haricot bean	lubya lbīḍa	لوبيا البيضا
hazelnut	nwāzeṭ	النوازيط
heart	qalb	قلب
hominy	ddrā maṣlūqa	الضرا مصلوقا
honey	^{c}assel	عسل

I

ice	thalzh	ثلج
ice cream	bāṣṭa/laglāṣṣ	باصطا\\الاچلاص
icing sugar	sukkar glaṣī	سكّر چلاصي
ingredient	qwām	قوام

J

Jalapeno chilli	ṣṣūdaniyya	سودانيا
jam	kunfitīr	كونفيتير
juice	^{c}aṣīr	عصير
juicer	^{c}aṣṣara	عصّارا
junket	Hlīb mrayyib	حليب مريّب

K

kettle	baqrāzh	بقراج
kidney	klāwi	كلاوي
kidney beans	lfūl lkhdar	الفول الخضر

kitchen	kuzīna/maṭbakh/kashshina	كوزين\مطبخ\كشينا
kiwi fruit	kīwi	كيوي
knife	sakkīn/mūs	سكّين\موس
knives	skākīn/mwās	سكاكن\مواس
kosher	kāshir	كاشير
kumquat	mzāH	مزاح

L

ladle	mghurfa	مغرفة
lamb	khrūf/ghanmi	خروف\غنمي
leek	būrru	بورّو
leg	zhigū	جيچو
lemon	lHamaḍ/limūn	الحامض\اليمون
lemonade	munāḍa bīḍa	موناضا بيضا
lime	limūn ddaq	ليمون الدّقّ
liqueur	likūr	ليكور
liver	kebda	كبدا
lobster	langūst	لنچوست
loin	buṣwīṭ	بوسويط
lunch	ghda	غدا

M

mackerel	mākru	ماكرو
main course	ṭazhīn	طاجين
mallow	baqqūla	بقّولا
mandarin	mandarin	ماندارين
mango	mang	مانچ
marinade	sharmūla	شرمولا
marinate	shermel	شرمل
marmalade	kunfitīr	كونفيتير
marrow	mukhkh	مخ
mayonnaise	mayyunīz	مايّونيز
meal	mākla	ماكلا
medium (cooked)	ṭayib mdāq	طايب مضاق
melon	battīkh/lmlūn	بتيخ\الملون
menu	menū	مينو
meringue	merāng	ميرانچ

milk	Hlīb	لحليب
mince	ṭaHHan	طحن
mincer	ṭaHHana	طحّانا
mineral water	ma' maᶜdini/ sidi ᶜali/ sidi Hrāzim	ماء معدن\ سيدي علي\ سيدي حرازم
mint	liqāma/naᶜnaᶜ	ليقاما\نعناع
morel	muriyy	موريي
mortar	mahrāz	مهراز
mussel	mūl	مول
mustard	muṭārḍ	موطارد
mutton	ghanmi	غنمي

N

napkin	mandīl	منديل
neck	ᶜanq	عنق
neck meat	ᶜangra	عنچرا
noodles	shaᶜriyya	شعريّا
nougat	nūga	نوچا
nut	gūz	چوز
nutcracker	hrrāst lgūz	هرّاست الچوز
nutmeg	gūzt ṭṭib	چوزة الطيب

O

offal	ssaqṭ	السّقط
oil	zīt	زيت
okra	mlūkhiyya	ملوخيا
olive (black)	zzītūn kHal	الزيتون كحل
olive (green)	zzītūn lkhḍar	الزيتون الخضر
olive oil	zīt zzītūn/ zīt lᶜud/	زيت الزيتو\ زيت العودن\
omelette	'umlīṭ	أومليط
orange	litchīn	ليتشين
oregano	zaᶜtar	زعتر
oven	farān	فران
oxtail	maghras	مغرس
oyster	maHHara	محّارا

P

papaya	papāya	بابايا
paprika	falfla Hamra	فلفلا حمرا
parasol	mḍall/baraṣūl	مضلّ\باراصول
parsley	mᶜadnūs	معدنوس
pasta	lepaṭ	ليباط
pastrami	ṣṣuṣīṣ	صوصيص
pastry	Halwa/ddwāz datāy	حلوى\الدواز د آتاي
peach	khūkh	خوخ
peanut	kāwkāw	كاوكاو
pears	ngāṣ/būᶜwīd	نجّاص\بوعويد
peas	zhalbāna	جلبانا
pecan	gūz pekān	چوز بيكان
pepper	falfla	فلفلا
persimmon	kāki	كاكي
pestle	yad lmahrāz	يد المهراز
to pickle	khallal/Hammaḍ	خلّل\حمّض
pickled	mṣayyer/mHammaḍ/ mkhallal	مصيّ\محمّض\ مخلّل
picnic	piknīc/nzāha	بيكنيك\نزاها
pigeon	Hmāma	حماما
pineapple	'ananās	آناناس
pistachio	pistāsh	بيستاش
plain flour	ṭHīn ᶜādi	طحين عادي
plate	ṭazhīn/ghṭār	طاجين\غطار
plum	barqūq	برقوق
plum tomatoes	maṭisha rumiyya	ماطيشا روميّا
poach	ṣlaq	صلق
pomegranate	rammān	رمان
popcorn	pupkorn	بوب كورن
pork	Hallūf/khanzīr	حلوف\خنزير
pot	ṭanzhra/ṭanzhiyya	طنجرا\طنجيّا
potato	baṭāṭā	باطاطا
potato masher	ṭaHHana dbaṭāṭā	طحّانا د باطاطا
prawn	krūvīt rwayāl	كروفيط روايال
preserves	mHammaḍ/mṣayyer	محمض\مصيير
pressure cooker	kokot minut	كوكوت مينوت
prune	barqūq	برقوق
pumpkin	qarᶜa lHamra	چرعا الحمرا

Q		
quail	Hzhel	لحجل
quince	sfarzhal	سفرجل
R		
rabbit	qniyya	قنيا
radish	lfzhal	الفجل
raisin	zbīb	زبيب
rare (cooked)	tāyib shwiyya	طايب شويّا
raspberry	frambowāz	فرامبواز
ray	rrāya	الرّايا
receipt	faktūra/risibu/ Hsāb	فاكتور\ريسيبو\ حسابا
red cabbage	krūm l'Hamar	الكرم الأحمر
red capsicum	lfalfla lHamra	الفلفلا الحمرا
red lentil	lᶜadess lHamra	العدس الحمرا
red onion	lbaṣla lHamra	البصلا الحمرا
reservation	lrizirvasyūn	الريزيرفاسيون
rhubarb	bārba	باربا
ribs	ḍluᶜ	ضلوع
rice	rrūzz	الروز
ripe	ṭayib	طايب
roast	mashwi	مشوي
rocket (lettuce)	shlāḍa rumiyya	شلاضا روميا
rockmelon	battīkh/sswihla/ lkantalū	بتيخ\السويهلة\ الكانطالو
rum	rrūm	الروم
rump	lmaghras	المغرس
S		
saffron	zaᶜfrān	زعفران
salad	shlāḍa	شلاضا
salad bowl	zlāfa d shlāḍa	زلافا د لشلاضا
salami	salāmi	سالامي
salmon	ṣumūn	صومون
salt	melHa	ملحا
sardine	sardīn	سردين
sauce	merqa/ṣūṣ	مرقا\صوص

saucepan	kāṣrūla	كاصرولا
sausage	ṣuṣīṣ	صوصيص
sauté	ṣuṭī	صوطي
savoury	ldīd/bnīn	لديبلنين
scales	mīzān	ميزان
scallop	liskalup	ليسكالوب
scissors	mqaṣ	مقص
sea carp	qurb	قرب
semolina	smīda	سميدا
service	srbīs/lpurbwār	سربيس\البوربوار
shallot	lizishalūṭ	ليزيشالوط
sharpening stone	maḍḍaya	مضايا
shoulder	ktaf	كتف
shrimp	qīmrūn/krūvīt	قمرون\كروفيت
sieve	gharbāl	غربال
simmer	bakhkhar	بخّر
sirloin	buftīk/fīlī	بوفتيك\فيلي
skewer	qṭīb d kābāb	قطيب د كاباب
smoke	bakhkhar	بخّر
snacks	kaskrūṭ	كاسكروط
snail	bubūsh/'aghlāl	بوبوش\أغلال
soft drink	munāḍa	موناضا
sole	ṣūl	صول
soup	ṣūbba	صوبا
soup spoon	mᶜalqa kbīra	معلقا كبيرا
soya bean	ṣṣūzha	الصوجا
spinach	lizipinār	ليزيبينار
spoon	mᶜalqa	معلقا
squash	qarᶜa lHamra	لچرعا الحمرا
squid	kālamār	كلامار
steak	sṭīk/lhabra	ستيك\الهبرا
steam	bakhkhar	بخّر
steamer	kaskās	كسكاس
stew	ṭayyib	طيّب
straw	lapāy	لابّاي
strawberry	frīz/ttūt rrūmi	لفريز\التوت الرومي
stuffing	ttaᶜmār	التعمار
sugar	sukar/sānida	سكر\سانيدا
sweet potatoes	baṭaṭa Hluwa	بطاطا حلوا

T

tablecloth	mandīl ṭṭabla	منديل الطبلا
tap water	lma' dl bazbūz	الماء دل بزبوز
tea	'atāy	أتاي
teaspoon	mᶜalqa sghīra	معلقا صغيرا
thyme	zaᶜtar	زعتر
tip	purbwār	بوربوار
toast	khubz mashwi	خبز مشوي
toaster	shawwāya d lkhubz	شوّايا د الخبز
tomatoes	maṭisha	ماطيشا
tongue	llsān	اللسان
tonic water	ṭonīk	طونيك
tripe	dewwāra	دوّارا
trout	laṭrwīt	لاطرويت
truffle	terfās	ترفاس
tuna	ṭūn	طون
turkey	bībi	بيبي
turnip	laft	لفت

V

vanilla	lavaniy	لاڤانيي
veal	ᶜzhal	لعجل
vegetables	khōḍār	خوضار
vinegar	khall	خل
vodka	vudka	ڤودكا

W

walnut	gūz/qarqaᶜ	چوز\چرچاع
water	ma'	ماء
watermelon	ddalāH	الدّلاّح
well done (cooked)	tāyib mezyān	طايب مزيان
wheat	zraᶜ /qamH	زرع\قمح
whisky	lwiskī	الويسكي
white cabbage	krūm byaḍ	كرم بيض
whiting	mīrla	ميرلا
wholewheat flour	ṭHīn d qamH	طحين د القمح
wild boar	ṣangliyyī	صانچلييي
wine	shshrāb/khamr	الشّراب\خمر
wooden spatula	mᶜalqa d lkhshab	معلقا د الخشب

Y		
yoghurt	yāgūr/dānun	ياچور\دانون
Z		
zucchini	qar^ca	لچرعا

The transliteration used in this dictionary contains symbols not found in the English alphabet (refer to the Pronunciation section for explanation).

We have included the symbols in this Eat Your Words section for accuracy but have left them out of the main text for ease of use.

At times, words commonly found in English, such as tajine and couscous, remain in these common forms in the main text, while they are given more accurate pronunciations here.

A

ᶜAcha عشا
meal during Ramaḍān

ᶜAchūra عاشورا
the 10th day of the Muslim Year/Festival of the children

ᶜadess عدس
(brown) lentil

ᶜadess lHamra عدس الحمرا
red lentil

ᶜadess lkhaḍra عدس الخضرا
green lentil

'aghlāl أغلال
snail

'agrish أچريش
remains of khliᶜ after cooking, generally beef together with **sharmūla** marinade. Very tasty. Used to make **rghāyif** or eaten with eggs.

ᶜaid/eid عيد
feast

ᶜAid el Kebir عيد الكبير
Festival of the Sacrifice of the Lamb

ᶜAid el Seghir عيد الصغير
religious festival ending of the Ramaḍān

ᶜain عَين
natural spring water

ᶜaish/ᶜaich عيش
paste-like mix of barley, salt and water, softer than **bazīn**

ᶜAit Souala عيت سوالا
wine variety - red

al-hamdū li-lLah الحمدُ لله
'thanks be to God'- prayer before eating

Allāh Akbar الله أكبر
'God the Great'

ᶜamalū عملو
delicious almond spread; argan oil (**zīt ᶜargan**) mixed with almond paste and honey

'ananās آناناس
pineapple

ᶜangra عنچرا
neck meat

ᶜanq عنق
neck

ᶜarach عرش
wood for chewing, to clean teeth

ᶜarq sūs عرق سوس
liquorice

ᶜaṣīḍa عصيضا
cooked semolina, served with honey, and usually prepared on the Aid el Molūd (the Prophet's birthday) for breakfast

ᶜaṣīr عصير
juice

ᶜaṣīr el mūz عصير الموز
a combination of milk and diced bananas

ᶜaṣīr ettuffaH عصير التفاح
a combination of milk and diced apples

ᶜaṣīr lfākya عصير الفاكيا
fruit juice

ᶜaṣīr mkhallaṭ عصير مخلّط
fruit punch

ᶜaṣīr ṭrī عصير طري
fresh juice

ᶜaṣṣara عصّارة
juicer

ᶜassel عسل
honey

'atāy أتاي
tea

ᶜaṭriyya عطرية
condiments

ᶜazhīna عجينا
batter

B

baba بابا
father

bābūr بابور
samovar, used for tea making

baghrīr بغرير
variety of pancakes, very light, made from fine semolina and flour, eaten for breakfast with butter and honey or khliᶜ on top

baguette (Fr.) باغيت
bread stick, long roll

bakhkhar بخّر
simmer/smoke/steam

balbūla بلبولا
barley; also barley semolina – a variety of couscous

baldi بلدي
cottage cheese

banāna بانانا
banana

banquette (Fr.) بانكيت
padded bench

baqqūla بقّولا
mallow (plant)

baqrāzh بقراج
kettle

baqri بقري
beef

baraṣūl باراصول
parasol

bārba باربا
beetroot/rhurbarb

barqūq برقوق
apricot/plum/prune

barrād برّاد
teapot

baṣla بصلا
onion

baṣla ʜamra بصلا لحمرا
red onion

bāṣṭa باصطا
ice cream

basṭīla بسطيلا
pounded pigeon, almonds, spices and creamy lemon flavoured eggs in Moroccan pastry – virtually the national dish (often made with chicken these days)

baṭāṭā باطاطا
potatoes

baṭāṭā ʜluwa بطاطا حلوا
sweet potatoes

baṭāṭā maqliyya بطاطا مقليّا
chips

baṭṭa بطّا
duck

battīkh بتيخ
cantaloupe/(rock)melon

bazhmāṭ بجماط
oval, crunchy, home baked biscuits, with anise and sesame seeds

bazīn بَزين
hard, paste-like mix of barley, salt and water (Libya)

bdanzhāl بادنجال
eggplant/aubergine

besbās بسباس
fennel

beshkīṭu بشكيطو
biscuits

bībi بيبي
turkey

bildī بلدي
bakehouse

bīrra بيرّا
beer/ale

biṣāra بيصارا
mashed dried broadbeans, served with cumin, red pepper and olive oil. Very popular and cheap dish

biskwī بيسكوي
biscuit

Bismillāh بسم الله
'in the name of God' – said before eating

bled بلِد
countryside

bnīn بنين
savoury

brāndi براندي
brandy

brik برك
deep-fried pastry triangles, stuffed with eggs, fish or **kefta** (Tunisian origin)

brioche (Fr.) بريوش
breakfast pastry

brīwāt بريوات
'little letters', small envelopes of flaky triangular shaped pastry, with sweet or savoury fillings and deep-fried in oil

brochette (Fr.) بروشيت
(see **kebāb**)

brokoli بروكولي
broccoli

bshkīṭu بشكيطو
cookies

bsībsa بسيبسا
mace

bubūsh بوبوش
snail

buftīk بوفتيك
sirloin

bulfāf بولفاف
seasoned grilled liver wrapped in caul (membrane); usually eaten on the first day of **Aid el Kebir**

būrru بورّو
leek/chives

buṣera بوصّيرة
tart bergamont lemons, preserved and used as a cooking ingredient

būṣwīṭ بوسويط
flank/loin

būᶜwīd بوعويد
pears

C

cafe au lait (Fr.) قهوة بالحليب
coffee with milk

congeles (Fr.) مثلّج
frozen food

couscous/seksū كُسكُسْ\سكسو
the traditional Moroccan dish, par excellence. Semolina, vegetables, and meat, are used to make **couscous**, which is usually eaten as a one-course family meal on Fridays, or supplements any gourmet meal. There are almost as many recipes for **couscous** in Morocco as there are cooks; and, of course, for everyone, their **couscous** is the best! It's the name of both the grain and cooked dish.

couscoussier (Fr.)/ kaskās كسكاس
couscous steamer (upper part)

crémerie (Fr.) كريمري
milk bar

D

ḍaffāya ضفّايا
ashtray

ḍalᶜa ضّلعة
chops

dalāн دّلاّح
watermelon

dānun دانون
yoghurt

demi-demi نص – نص
half strength coffee

dewwāra دوّارا
lambs tripe & innards simmered in a hot spicy sauce, usually eaten during **Aid el Kebir**

ḍīffa ضّيفة
banquet; couscous is always served at the end of **ḍīffa** to make sure no guests are left hungry

dirham درهم
money unit

dissīr ديسير
dessert

djellāba جلاّبة
tailored street-length hooded cloak, worn by men and women

dlākrīm دلاكريم
cream cheese

dlmaᶜza دالمعزة
goat's cheese

ḍluᶜ ضلوع
ribs

doHi ضوحي
midday prayer

doqq دوق
very small lemons that are highly prized; preserved in salt

drā دّرا
corn

drā maṣlūqa درا مصلوقا
cornmeal (hominy)

drā ṣghīra درا صّغيرا
baby corn

dwāz d'atāy دواز د آتاي
cakes, pastry

dzhāzh دجاج
chicken

dzhāzh msharmal دجاج مشرمل
chicken **ṭāzhin** with olives and preserved lemons where sauce is flavoured with saffron, ginger and pepper

E

epicerie أبيسري
general store, small supermarket

F

faktūra فاكتورا
receipt

fākya فاكيا
fruit

fākya d lmuluk فاكيا د الملوك
'king's fruit', almond pastry, shaped like a pear, an apple, or other fruit, dipped in food colouring

fākya yābsa فاكيا يابسا
dried fruit

falfla فلفلا
capsicum/chilli/pepper

falfla Hamra فلفلا حمرا
paprika/red capsicum

falfla Harra فلفلا حرّا
hot chilli

falfla Hluwa فلفلا حلوّا
sweet chilli

falfla sudāniyya فلفلا سودانيّا
very hot chilli

fanīd فنيد
candy

faqqāṣ فقّاص
oval, crunchy, homebaked biscuits, with anise and sesame seeds

faqquṣ فقّوص
variety of cucumber – often grated and served as a delicious and refreshing summer salad with sugar, orange blossom water and thyme

farān فران
oven

farūj/dujay/ poulet (Fr.) فروج\ دجاي\ دجاج
chicken

fasūliya فاصوليا
haricot beans (white)

fegg^c^a فچّاع
mushrooms

feṭrā فطرا
a mixture of equal parts of the grains wheat, barley and corn

fīlī فيلي
fillet, sirloin

fliyyu فليّو
wild mint

frambowāz فرامبواز
raspberry

frīt فريت
fried potatoes/chips

friteries (Fr.) فريتري
fried food shops

frīz فريز
strawberry

frumazh فرماج
cheese

fṭūr فطور
breakfast

fūl gnāwa فول چناوا
black(-eyed) bean

fūl lkbīr فول الكبير
red kidney bean

funūy فونوي
fennel

fursheṭa فورشيطا
fork

fzhal فجل
radish

G

garnina چرنينا
thistle stem

ghadā غدا
lunch

ghalla غلّا
to boil

ghanmi غنمي
lamb/mutton

gharbāl غربال
sieve

ghriyyba غريّبا
small, round cake, usually made of fine semolina, but can also be made of coconut and crushed sesame seeds

ghṭār غطار
plate

gris (Fr.) غريس
'grey' - light red wine

griwash چريواش
flour, sesame and egg based pastry, fried in honey, and eaten

mostly during the holy month of **Ramaḍān** to accompany **Hrira**

gūz چوز
nut

gūz pekān چوز باكان
pecan

gūzt ṭṭib چوزة الطيب
nutmeg

H

Habb lmlūk حبّ الملوك
cherries

Habbat Hlawa حبّة حلاوا
green Spanish aniseed

Hakk حك
to grate

Hallala حلالة
bottle/can opener

Hallūf حلوف
pork

Halwa حلوا
cakes/pastry/sweets

Halwa blfākya حلوا بالفاكيا
fruit cake

Halwa d ddrā حلوا د الدّرا
cornmeal

Halwa rghāyif حلوا ﻏايف
cone shaped honey cake, served with fresh butter, mainly at special ceremonies

Hamaḍ حامض
lemon

hamburger هامبورچر
hamburger

Ham ḍḍalᶜa حم الضلعا
brisket

Ham l Hallūf حم الحلّوف
bacon

Hammaḍ حمّض
to pickle

Hammām حمّام
public steam bath

Hammūṣ حمّص
chickpeas

handiyya هنديّا
prickly pears

harissa هريسا
fiery hot sauce; a rich chilli paste, red in colour

Harsha حرشا
type of semolina pancake

Hawamiḍ حوامض
citrus

hegīra هجيرة
new year festival

hergma هرچمة
feet (calf or sheep), prepared with chickpeas and crushed wheat

herrbel هرّبل
crushed wheat cooked in milk

hijra هجرة
islamic year

hindīr هندير
prickly pear

Hlīb حليب
milk

Hlīb mrayyib حليب مريّب
junket, usually prepared with **nyāhq**

Hmāma حماما
pigeon

Hrira حريرا
thick, very rich soup, with chickpeas, lentils, meat and coriander. It's eaten as a meal in itself or as a starter. Often used to break the fast during **Ramaḍān**.

hrrāst lgūz هرّاست الچوز
nutcracker

Hrūr حرور
chilli

Hsāb حساب
bill/cheque/receipt

Hūt حوت
fish

Hūt bū-eṭob حوت بوالطب
fish stuffed with dates

Hzhel حجل
pheasant/quail

I

ifṭār إفطار
the breaking of the fast at sundown during **Ramaḍān**

ᶜinab عنب
grapes

J

jemil جمل
camel

jus de banana (Fr.)
(*see* **ᶜaṣīr el mūz**)

jus de pommes (Fr.)
(*see* **ᶜaṣīr ettūffaH**)

K

kaᶜb ghzāl كعب غزال
'gazelles' horns or ankles; pastry crescents filled with almond paste and served with fresh dates

kāki كاكي
persimmon

kālamār كلامار
squid

kammūn كمون
cumin

kanṭalū كانطالو
cantaloupe

kāramil كراميل
caramel

karwiyya كرويا
caraway seeds

kāshir كاشير
kosher; also pre-cooked sausage, made of meat or chicken (no pork), widely used for sandwiches and light snacks

kashshina كشّينا
kitchen

kaskrūṭ كاسكروط
snacks

kāṣrūla كاصرولا
saucepan

kāvyār كافيار
caviar

kāwkāw كاوكاو
peanut

kāwkāw rrumi كاوكاو الرّومي
cashew

kebāb كباب
bits of grilled meat on a skewer; beef, veal, lamb or mutton can be used, as well as offal; also called **brochette** (Fr.)

kebda كبدا
liver

kefta كفتا
seasoned minced lamb

kefta mqawara كفتا مقوّرة
kefta ṭāzhin served with tomato and eggs

kelīm قليم
type of textile

keneffa كنافة
deep-fried thin pastry interspersed with a crunchy mix of ground almonds, icing sugar and powdered cinnamon

kermūṣ كرموص
fig; also eggplant puree cooked with tomatoes

kermus nnṣāra كرموص النّصارا
prickly pears

kesra كسرا
bread made in wood-fired ovens

khabya خابية
large earthenware jars used to preserve foods to last the year or to churn butter in

khadra خضرا
legumes/vegetables

khall خلّ
vinegar

khallal خلّل
to pickle

khamr خمر
wine

khanzīr خنزير
pork

kharshūf خرشوف
cardoon; thick stemmed vegetable which needs slow cooking to reduce the bitterness

khbaz خبز
bake

khess (laitue, Fr.) خس
lettuce

khōḍār خوضار
vegetables

khrūf خروف
lamb

khubz/khobz خبز
bread

khubz mashwi خبز مشوي
toast

khudra خوضار
ingredient in **baṣṭīla**

khūkh خوخ
peach

khyār خيار
cucumber

khzāma خزاما
lavender

kīf كيف
cannabis/hashish

kiwi كيوي
kiwifruit

klāwi كلاوي
kidney

klīla كليلة
cottage cheese

kokot minut كوكوت مينوت
pressure cooker

krab كراب
crab

krachel كراشل
biscuit variety; small, sweet bread rolls flavoured with aniseed and sprinkled with sesame seeds

krāffṣ كرافص
celery

krūm كروم
cabbage

krūm byāḍ كروم بيض
white cabbage

krūm l'ʜmar كروم الأحمر
red cabbage

krūm ṣṣghīr كروم الصّغير
bok choy/chinese cabbage

krūvīt كروفيت
shrimp

krūvīt rwayāl كروفيط روايال
prawn

krwaṣṣa كرواصّا
croissant

Kseksū Bidawi كسكْسو بدوي
'**Couscous** with Seven Vegetables': cabbage, carrots, pumpkin, peas, artichoke hearts, turnips, sweet potatoes or any vegetable in season

ktaf كتف
shoulder

kubbār كبّار
capers

kuka kula كوكاكولا
coke

kukṭil كوكتيل
cocktail

kūkū كوكو
coconut

kunfitīr كونفيتير
jam/marmalade

kuri كوري
curry

kuri madquq كوري مدقوق
curry powder

kurn flīks كورن فليكس
cornflakes

kurnishon كورنيشون
gherkin

kuṭlīṭ كوتليت
cutlet

kuzīna كوزينا
kitchen

kwāʜ كواح
small cubes of mutton fat and liver, marinated and grilled on skewers

L

lādition لاديسيون
bill/cheque

laft لفت
turnip

laglaṣ لاكلاص
ice cream

lakrim لاكريم
cream

lāmurī لاموري
cod

lāngust لنكوست
lobster

lanshwa لانشوا
anchovy

lanṭri لانطري
appetiser/entree

lapāy لابّاي
straw

lāpiritif لابيتيف
aperitif

laranj لرانج
bitter oranges used to prepare olives and other preserves (not for eating)

larnab لرنب
hare

laṣūṣ لاصوص
broth

laṭrwīt لاطرويت
trout

laurier اللوريي
bay leaves

lavaniy لافانيي
vanilla

lāvukā لافوكا
avocado

lben اللبن
buttermilk

lbīḍ البيض
eggs

lblū لبلو
blue cheese

ldīḍ لديد
savoury

lehem/agneau (Fr.) لحم خروف
lamb

lehem/viande (Fr.) لحم
meat

lehem jemil لحم جمل
camel meat

lepaṭ ليباط
pasta

lhabra الهبرا
steak

libzār البزار
pepper (spice)

līkur ليكور
liqueur

līmūn ليمون
small green Moroccan lemons (not quite lemons and not really limes)

līmun ddaq ليمون الدّقّ
lime

līmun lmerr/ الّيمون المرّ\
līmun mṣayyar ّليمون المصيّر
bitter lemon

liqāma ليقاما
mint

lishū d bruksīl ليشو د بروكسيل
brussels sprouts

liskalup ليسكالوب
scallop

litchīn ليتشين
orange

litshi ليتشي
lychee

lizandīv ليلزنديف
endive

lizasperzh ليزاسبيرج
asparagus

lizipinār ليزيبينار
spinach

lizishalūṭ ليزيشالوط
shallot

lkhashba الخشبة د
dttaqt^{c}ā التقطاع
chopping board

lkhmīra الخميرا
baking soda

lmākla d lHkak الماكلا د الحكاك
conserves

lqīm اللقيم
spring apples, used to make one of the most delicious **ṭāzhin**, usually with mutton

lranzh اللرانج
bitter lemon, used to prepare olives and other preserves (not for eating)

lsān لسان
tongue

l^{c}sha العشا
dinner

lūbya لوبيا
bean

lūbya lbīḍa لوبيا البيضا
haricot bean (white)

lūz لوز
almond

lwezz الوزّ
goose

lwiskī الويسكي
whisky

lwiza اللويزا
verbena – bittersweet herb used in tea

M

mā' ماء
water

mā' dl bazbūz ماء دل البزبوز
tap water

mā' m^{c}adini ماء معدني
sparkling mineral water

madāq مداق
flavour

maḍḍaya مضّايا
sharpening stone

m^{c}adnūs معدنوس
parsley/angelica

maghras مغرس
oxtail/rump

Maghreb مغرب
west, literally where the sun sets – Morocco, Algeria and Tunisia

Maghrebiyya مغربية
couscous from Maghreb, Nth Africa

maghzal مغزل
metal kebab skewer

maHHara محّارا
oyster

mahrāz مهراز
brass mortar and pestle, used to pound spices, herbs and grains

majūn معجون
'hash cookie', candied fruit

majmar مجمر
charcoal brazier, usually round and made of unglazed pottery

majmaroli مجمرولي
majmar cooker pot

mākina dl qahwa ماكنا د القهوا
coffee machine

mākla ماكلا
meal

mākru ماكرو
mackerel

mᶜalqa معلقا
spoon

mᶜalqa d ddissīr معلقا د الدّيسير
dessert spoon

mᶜalqa d lkhshab معلقا د الخشب
wooden spatula

mᶜalqa kbīra معلقا كبيرا
soup spoon

mᶜalqa sghīra معلقا صغيرا
teaspoon

malwi ملوى
variety of pancake, similar to **rghāyif**

mandarin ماندارين
mandarin

mandīl ṭṭabla منديل الطبلا
tablecloth

mandīl منديل
napkin

mang مانچ
mango

manyok مانيوك
polenta

maqla مقلا
frying pan

maqla d shshinwa مقلا د الشينوا
wok

maqla dyāl ṭrāb مقلي ديال طراب
large, round earthenware plate

maqlī مقلي
deep-fried

mardashūsh مردشّوش
marjoram

marqa مرقا
gravy

Marrakshiya مكراشية

mashmāsh مشماش
apricot

mashrūbāt مشروبات
drinks

mashwī/meshwī مشوي
whole roast lamb or sheep on the spit

maṭbakh مطبخ
kitchen

maṭisha ماطيشا
tomatoes

maṭisha rumiyya ماطيشا روميّاً
plum tomatoes

māṭisha sghīra ماطيشا صغيرا
cherry tomatoes

mayyunīz مايّونيز
mayonnaise

mazhmar مجمر
barbeque grill

mazzāH مزّاح
kumquat

mḍall مضلّ
parasol

medīna مدينة
'old' quarter

mekhtamrīn مختمرين
fried filled puff pastry

melHa ملحا
salt – also the Jewish quarter of the **medīna**

menū مينو
menu

merāng مرانج
meringue

merqa مرقا
broth/sauce

merqa lmqallya مرقا المقلّيا
brown sauce

meska مسكا
gum arabic – vegetable gum used to thicken dishes

msellāla مسّلالا
variety of preserved green olives, left for several days in water and salt to lose some of their bitter taste

mghurfa مغرفة
ladle

mHammaḍ محمّض
pickled/preserves

mHammar محمّر
red sauce, with butter, sweet paprika, and cumin as base

mHammṣa محمّصا
coarse rolled wheat grains, steamed to make one variety of couscous, or cooked in sauce to make soup

mHannsha محنّشا
coiled serpent cake, a flat round of baked almond-stuffed pastry, dusted with icing sugar and cinnamon

mHekka محكا
grater

miksūr ميكسور
blender

mīrla ميرلا
whiting

mīzān ميزان
scales

mkhallal مخلّل
pickled

mlūkhiyya ملوخيّا
okra – delicous vegetable with a slimy texture

mlūn ملون
melon

Molūd مولود
Festival of the birthday of the Prophet

mqalli مقلّي
yellow sauce with oil, saffron, and ginger

mqaṣ مقص
scissors

mrayyib-rrāyib مريّب، الرّايب
traditional, homemade yoghurt, made with the hearts of Moroccan artichokes. These days popularly sold in **crémeries**

mruziyya مروزيّا
sweet and sour **ṭāzhin**, with mutton, raisins, almonds, a rich blend of spices including **Ras-el-Hanūt** in a thick brown sauce. Can be kept for over a month without refrigeration

mṣayyer مصيّر
preserves/pickled

msharmal مشرمل
red sauce made from saffron, ginger, oil, onions, peppers, and cumin

mukhkh مخ
brain/marrow

mūl مول
mussel

munāḍa موناضا
soft drink

munāḍa bīḍa موناضا بيضا
lemonade

muriyy موريي
morel

mūs موس
knife

muṭārḍ موطارد
mustard

mūz لموز
banana

myādi ميادي
simple, rimmed round tables

mwās مواس
knives

mzāн مزاح
kumquat

N

nāfa^{c} نافع
anise

ngāṣ نجاص
pears

nakhāla نخّالا
bran

na^{c}na^{c} نعناع
mint

nbaq نبق
currant

ness ness نص نص
half coffee half milk (half half)

nfissāt نفيسات
thin nourishing mutton soup

nūga نوكا
nougat

nwa نّوا
almonds

nwāzeṭ نـوازيـط
hazelnut

nyāq نّـيـاق
wild artichoke beard, used to curdle milk

nzāha نـزاهـا
picnic

P

pamplumūs بـامـبـلـومـوس
grapefruit

papāya بـابـايـا
papaya

pastis (Fr.) بـاسـتـيـس
aniseed-based spirit

patisserie (Fr.) بـاتـيـسـري
cake and pastry shop

piknīc بـيـكـنـيـك
picnic

pistāsh بـيـسـتـاش
pistachio

poisson (Fr.) حـوت
fish

poulet (Fr.) دجـاج
chicken

pupkorn بـوب كـورن
popcorn

purbwār بـوربـوار
tip, service

Q

qadra قـدرا
yellow sauce, made from butter, onions, pepper, and saffron (the lightest among Moroccan basic sauces)

qahwa قـهـوة
coffee

qahwa-ʜlīb قـهـوة حـلـيـب
coffee with milk, white coffee

qahwa-keʜla قـهـوة كـحـلا
black coffee

qahwa-mherresa قـهـوة مـهـرّسـة
coffee ‘broken’ with a splash of milk

qahwa-mher قـهـوة مـهـر
weak, mostly milk, ‘broken’ with a little coffee

qalb قـلـب
heart

qamʜ قـمـح
wheat

qannariyya قـنّـاريّـا
cardoon; thick stemmed vegetable which needs slow cooking to reduce the bitterness

qa^c qulla قـاع قـلا
cardamon

qar^{c}a قـرعـا
courgette/zucchini

qar^{c}a lʜamra قـرعـا لـحـمـرا
pumpkin/squash

qar^{c}a slawiya قـرعـا سـلاويّـا
large, long, light green variety of squash

qar^{c}a takhrifīn قـرعـا تـاخـيـفـيـن
butternut squash

qarqā^c قـرقـاع
walnut

qaṣ^{c}a قـصـعـا
deep rectangular dish, made of earthenware or wood, used to

prepare bread, knead dough, or serve **couscous**

qarfa قرفة
cinnamon

qarqūb قرقوب
turmeric (curcuma)

qaṭᶜa قطعا
aperitif

qeṣbūr قصبور
coriander

qesṭāl قسطال
chestnut

qeṭṭāra قطارة
distiller for distilling flower water

qīmrūn قمرون
shrimp

qiṣṣarya قصاريا
covered market

qli قلي
fry/deep-fry

qniyya قنيا
rabbit

qrunfal قرنفل
clove

qṭīb d kābāb قطيب د كاباب
skewer

qūq قوق
wild artichoke: a variety with striking spiky leaves – both stalks and flower head eaten

qūq baldi قوق بلدي
Jerusalem Artichoke, wild artichoke

qūq d shshūk قوق د الشوك
(*see* **quq baldi**)

qurb قرب
sea carp

qwām قوام
ingredient

R

Ramaḍān رمضان
9th month of Muslim year, a period of fasting during the day

rammān رمان
pomegranate

Rās-el-Hanūt راس الحانوت
'shopkeeper's choice' – a mixture of spices

rbāya رباية
tea cannister

rghāyif غايف
variety of pancakes, either eaten spicy and stuffed with onions and khliᶜ (or other type of meat) or plain with sugar or honey

risibu ريسيبو
receipt

rizirvasyun الريزيرفاسيون
reservation

robo d lkuzina روبو د الكوزينا
food processor

rotisseries (Fr.) روتيسري
roast chicken fast food outlets

rrāy الراي
rai, modern Algerian dance music

rrāya الرّايا
ray

rrayib الرّايب
traditional, homemade yoghurt

rrūm الروم
rum

rrūzz الروز
rice

rrūzz rrūmi الروز الرّومي
basmati rice/brown rice

S

ṣāfi, baraka صافي، بركة
enough, 'no thank you'

sakkīn سكّين
knife

salade marocaine (Fr.) شلاضا مغربية
Moroccan salad

salmiya ساليّا
sage

sallū سلّو
dark brown pastry with flour, sugar, almonds, sesame seeds, anis, all crushed and dry fried, eaten with spoon during **Ramaḍān** or upon the birth of a child

ṣamta صّمطا
eel

ṣandriyyi صاندرييّي
ashtray

ṣangliyyī صانچلييي
wild boar

sānida سانيدا
sugar

saqṭ سّقط
offal

sardīn سردين
sardine

seffa سفّا
couscous semolina, steamed, and served dry (no sauce or vegetables) with powdered sugar, cinnamon and milk. Usually eaten for dinner

sellu سلّو
dark brown pastry with flour, sugar, almonds, sesame seeds, and anise, all crushed and dry fried. It's very rich in calories and usually prepared during **Ramaḍān** or to celebrate the birth of a child.

serruda سرّودا
mashed dried chickpeas, served with onion, butter, and saffron. Very popular and cheap dish.

sfarzhal سفرجل
quince

sfenzh سفنج
doughnuts/fritters

shᶜīr شعير
barley

shabᶜaān شبعان
complete satiation

shābal شابل
bass

shabbakiya شبّاك
flour, sesame and egg based pastry, fried in honey, and eaten mostly during the holy month of **Ramaḍān**

shāf شاف
chef

shahdiya شهديّا
peach plum; a variety of summer fruit which is a cross between plums and peaches, and tastes of both

shaнma شحما
grease

shampanya شامبانيا
champagne

shampinyun شامبينيون
mushroom

sharbāt شرابات
fruit and/or nut drink

sharbāt billūz شرابات باللوز
almond milk – a lusciously rich and creamy drink with a fragrant taste

shaᶜriyya شعريّا
noodles/vermicelli

sharmel شرمل
marinate

sharmūla شرمولة
marinade for fish, chicken or **brochettes** of lamb

shashnu شاشنو
local variety of wild orange berries, about the size of strawberries

shawwāya d lkhubz شوّايا د الخبز
toaster

sherba شربا
spicy soup (Libya)

shklāṭ شكلاط
chocolate

shlāḍa شلاضا
salad/appetiser

shlāḍa rumiyya شلاضا روميا
rocket (lettuce)

shība شيبة
absinth

shīkurī شيكوري
chicory

shrāb شراب
wine/alcoholic sodas

shwā شوا
barbeque

shṭūn شطون
anchovy

shūflūr شوفلور
cauliflower

shūka شوكا
fork

ṣhūr صحور
meal during **Ramaḍān** before sunrise

shwa شّوا
barbecued whole sheep (or half sheep), usually served in ceremonies, and eaten with salt and cumin

shwī شوي
braise/grill

sīdī سيدي
Mr/honourific title

sidi ᶜali/ سيدي حرازم\
sidi нrazim سيدي علي،
mineral water brands, widely used – **sidi ᶜali** has almost acquired a generic sense

sikūk سيكوك
variety of **couscous**, eaten dry, without vegetables or meat, but with butter milk and steamed fava beans

sīlri سيلري
celery

ṣiniyya صينيّا
round (or rectangular) tray, made of copper or brass, used in tea preparation ceremony

skākīn سكاكن
knives

skīn zhbīr سكينجبير
ginger

ṣlaq صلق
poach

smen سمن
preserved, melted and salted butter, with a rather strong taste, used mainly in cooking

smīda سميدا
semolina

sakkūm سكوم
asparagus

salāmi سالامي
salami

ṣder صدر
breast

sidr سيدر
cider

sīryāl سيريال
cereal

srbīs سربيس
service

sṭīk ستيك
steak

sūdaniyya سودانيا
cayenne/Jalapeno chilli

sūdaniyya ṣghīra سودانيّا صغيرا
bird's eye chilli

sukkar سكر
sugar

sukkar glaṣi سكر چلاصي
icing sugar

sūq سوق
souk/market

ṣuṣīṣ صوصيص
chorizo/sausage/frankfurter/pastrami

ṣuṭī صوطي
sauté

ṣūzha صوجا
soya bean

swihla سويهلة
cantaloupe

ṣūbba صوبا
soup

ṣūbba d lḥūt صّوبّا د الحوت
fish chowder

ṣūl صول
sole

ṣumūn صومون
salmon

Sunna سنّة
Mohammedan traditions

ṣūṣ صوص
sauce

T

ṭabac (Fr.) تباك
tobacconist/newsagency

tafrīq تفريق
post-funeral meal

ṭaghra طغرة
Berber ṭāzhin (Rif Mountains)

ṭaHHan طحن
mince

ṭaHHana طحّانا
blender/mixer/mincer

ṭaHHana dbaṭaṭa طحّانا د باطاطا
potato masher

ṭaHHana dl qahwa طحّانا د القهوا
coffee grinder

ṭaHHana thūm طحّانا ثوم
garlic press

taᶜmār تعمار
stuffing

tamra تمرة
date

ṭanzhīr طنجير
very large boiling pot, used to cook khliᶜ in very large quantities at a time (up to 50 kilos or even more)

ṭanzhiyya طنجيّا
'a bachelor's dish' – cooked in a two handled earthenware vessel. The cook has no need of kitchen or stove as it's taken to the **hammām** to cook on the ashes for 8 hours.

ṭanzhra طنجرا
pot, aluminium or other metal, more widely used than the **ṭanzhiyya**

ṭaṣa طّاسا
cup

ṭayib طايب
ripe

ṭayib mezyān طايب مزيان
well done (cooked)

ṭayib mdāq طايب مضاق
medium (cooked)

ṭayib shwiyya طايب شويّا
rare (cooked)

ṭayyib طيّب
stew

ṭāzhin/ṭājīne طاجين
stews cooked in the dish of the same name – a round earthenware dish with pointed lid, used to cook food. Sometimes refers to typical Moroccan dishes, whether cooked in a **ṭāzhin** or not.

ṭāzhin/ṭājīne slāwi طاجين سلاوي
vegetable lamb **ṭāzhin** where the slawi vegetable (pale green from the squash family) is used to give a subtle flavour; also a round flameproof dish of earthenware with a pointed glazed earthenware cover, used to cook **ṭāzhins** or stews

ṭbaq طباق
colourful large straw baskets, decorated with leather, with pointed lids to keep bread fresh; also large flat basket used to roll or separate semolina grains for **couscous**

terfās ترفاس
truffle

terfās byāḍ ترفاس بيض
white truffle

terfās kHal ترفاس كحل
black truffle

tfaya تفايا
meat dish, in a brownish sauce (coriander, saffron, pepper, and onion), served with grilled almonds and boiled eggs

thalzh ثلج
ice

tHāmaḍ تحامض
bitters

thé or 'atāy Lipton أتاي
'English' tea (usually served without milk)

thé marocaine (Fr.)/ atāy طبصيل\ ديال ورقة
Moroccan tea; mint tea

ṭHīn طحين
flour

ṭHīn ᶜādi طحين عادي
plain flour

ṭHin d ddrā طحين الدّرا
cornmeal

ṭHīn d gamH طحين د القمح
wholewheat flour

thūm ثوم
garlic

tisane زهورات
mint and water infusion, other herbs can be used

tmer لتمر
dates

ṭobṣil زهورات
large, low, circular pan or plate

ṭobṣil dyāl warqa
طبصيل ديال ورقة
round flat metal dish with at shallow rim, used to make **warqa** pastry

ṭonīk طونيك
tonic water

ṭraH طرح
bake

trīd تريد
sweet and spicy, very thin layers of fried dough, stuffed with eggs, meat, chicken, or pigeon, and served with cinnamon and sugar. Favourite dish of the Prophet

tships تشيبس
chips

tshīsha تشيشا
burghul (cracked wheat); also the light soup, made of finely crushed wheat cooked in a spicy broth with tomatoes and pepper

tuffāH تفاح
apple

ṭūn طون
tuna

tūt توت
berries

tūt l'arḍ توت الأرض
blueberry/cranberry/dewberry

tūt rrūmi توت الرّومي
blackberry/gooseberry/strawberry

U

'umlīṭ أومليط
omelette

V

vudka فودكا
vodka

W

warqa ورقة
thin pastry similar to filo, the vital ingredient in **basṭīla**

wrāq sidna mūsa وراق سيدنا موسى
bay leaves

Y

yad lmahrāz يد المهراز
pestle

yāgūr ياكور
yoghurt

Z

zaᶜfrān زعفران
saffron; dried stigmas of Crocus Sativus used for colour and distinctive flavour

zaᶜtar زعتر
oregano-like wild herb from the scrubby wastes of the pre-Sahara

zaaluk زعلوك
eggplant (aubergine), zucchini (courgette), and tomato salad, all cooked in oil with red and hot peppers – served as a starter

zafzuf زفزوف
local variety of currant, larger and sweeter than **nbaq**

zarriᶜt lfunūy زريعة لفونوي
fennel seed

zbīb زبيب
raisin

zebda زبدا
butter

zhaban جابان
candy, prepared with gum arabic (*see* **meska**) and crushed roasted almonds

zhabbaniya جبّانيّا
bowl

ᶜzhal لعجل
veal

zhalbāna جلبانا
peas

zhambūn جامبون
ham

zhben جبن
cheese

zhenzhlān جنجلان
sesame seed

zhigu جيچو
leg

zhrāna جرانا
frog

zīt زيت
oil

zīt ᶜargan زيت عرچن
highly flavoured oil extracted from the nuts of the argan trees, used in salads and some sweets

zīt lᶜud/ زيت العود\
zīt zītūn زيت الزيتون
olive oil

zītūn زيتون
olive – a key ingredient or garnish in Moroccan dishes

zītūn kHal زيتون كحل
black olive

zītūn lkhḍar زيتون الخضر
green olive

zlāfa زلافا
bowl

zlāfa d shlāḍa زلافا د الشلاضا
salad bowl

zraᶜ زرع
wheat

zraᶜ mharmash زّرع مهرمش
cracked wheat

FRENCH

Pronunciation

French is widely spoken in Morocco, so it can be useful to have a few words at hand. As transliterations can only give an approximate guide to pronunciation, here's a guide for those who want to try pronouncing French more accurately.

Vowels

a	as the 'u' in 'cup'
e	barely pronounced, as the 'e' in 'open'
é	as the 'ay' in 'may'
è	as the 'e' in 'merry', but slightly longer
i	as in 'hit'
o	as in the British 'pot'
u	to make this sound, purse your lips as if you were saying 'oo' but make the sounds 'ee'

Diphthongs

ai	as the 'e' in 'bet' but a bit longer
eu	as the 'er' in the British 'berth' but shorter
oi	sounds like 'wa'
ui	sounds like 'wi'
au	as the 'o' in 'or'
eau	as the 'ow' in 'show'
ou	as the 'oo' in 'book'

Nasal Vowels

During the production of nasal vowels the breath escapes partly through the nose and partly through the mouth. There are no nasal vowels in English; in French they occur where a syllable ends in a single n, m or nt: the last consonants are not pronounced, but indicate the nasalisation of the preceding vowel. They sound approximately like this:

on	nasal 'o', the vowel as in 'pose'
in	nasal 'u', the vowel as in 'cup'
an	nasal 'o', the vowel as in 'hot'

Consonants & Semiconsonants

c	hard, like 'k' before 'a', 'o' or 'u'
ç	always soft, like 's'
g	hard, as in 'get', before 'a', 'o' and 'u'
	soft, as in 'germ', before 'e' and 'i'
h	always silent
j	as the ;s' in 'measure'
l	always pronounced with the tip of the tongue touching the back of the upper incisors, and the surface of the tongue higher than for an English 'l'.
q	as the 'k' in 'king'.

r	the standard 'r' is produced by moving the bulk of the tongue backwards to constrict the air flow in the pharynx, while the tip of the tongue rests behind the lower front teeth. It is quite similar to the noise made by some people before spitting, but with much less friction. For those who know Spanish, it is like the jota, except that it is 'softer' and voiced.
s	as the 's' in 'sit', except between two vowels when it is pronounced as 'z'

Top Useful Phrases

Hello.	**bõ-zhoor**	*Bonjour.*
Goodbye.	**oh rer-vwar**	*Au revoir.*
Yes/No.	**wee/nõ**	*Oui/Non.*
Excuse me.	**ehk-skü-ze mwa**	*Excusez-moi.*
Please.	**seel voo pleh**	*S'il vous plaît.*
Thank you.	**mehr-see**	*Merci.*
Many thanks.	**mehr-see boh-koo**	*Merci beaucoup.*
Sorry. (excuse me, forgive me)	**par-dõ**	*Pardon.*
That's fine.	**treh byen**	*Très bien.*
You're welcome.	**zher voo zã pree**	*Je vous en prie.*

Greetings

Good morning/afternoon.	**bõ-zhoor**	*Bonjour.*
Good evening/night.	**bõ-swar**	*Bonsoir.*
How are you?	**ko-mã ta-le voo?**	*Comment allez-vous?*
Well, thanks.	**byen mehr-see!**	*Bien, merci!*

Crossing the Language Barrier

Do you speak English?
voo par-le ã-gle? — *Vous parlez anglais?*

Does anyone speak English?
ehs-keel-ya kehl-ken kee parl ã-gle? — *Est-ce qu'il y a quelqu'un qui parle anglais?*

I speak a little French.
zher parl en per der frã-se — *Je parle un peu de français.*

I (don't) understand.
zher (ner) kõ-prã (pa) — *Je (ne) comprends (pas).*

Could you speak more slowly?
eh-sker voo poo-rye par-lei plü lã-tmã? — *Est-ce que vous pourriez parler plus lentement?*

Food

breakfast	**ler per-tee de-zher-ne**	*le petit déjeuner*
lunch	**ler de-zher-ne**	*le déjeuner*
dinner	**ler dee-ne**	*le dîner*

Eating Out

Table for ..., please.
ün tabl poor ... pehr-son, seel voo ple — *Une table pour ... personnes, s'il vous plaît.*

Can I see the menu please?
ehs-ker zher per vwar lah kart? — *Est-ce que je peux voir la carte?*

I'd like the set lunch, please.
zher prã ler mer-nü — *Je prends le menu.*

Is service included in the bill?
ehs-ker ler sehr-vees e kõ-pree? — *Est-ce que le service est compris?*

Do you accept credit cards?
proh-ne-voo leh kart dü kre-dee — *Prenez-vous les cartes de crédit?*

an ashtray	**en sã-dree-ye**	*un cendrier*
the bill/check	**lah-dee-syõ**	*l'addition*
a cup	**ün tas**	*une tasse*
dessert	**ler de-sehr**	*le dessert*
a drink	**ün bwah-sõ**	*une boisson*
a glass	**en vehr**	*un verre*
toothpick	**en kür dã**	*un cure-dent*

Vegetarians

I'm a vegetarian.
zher swee vei-zhe-tar-yã/ ve-zhe-tar-yehn — *Je suis végétarien (m)/* végétarienne (f).

I don't eat meat.
zher ner mãzh pah der vyãd — *Je ne mange pas de viande.*

I don't eat chicken, fish or ham.
zher ner mãzh pa der poo-le, der pwa-sõ oo der zhã-bõ — *Je ne mange pas de poulet, de poisson ou de jambon.*

Reading the Menu

Viandes et Volailles	Meat & Poultry
canard	duck
contrefilet	sirloin roast
dinde/dindon/dindonneau	turkey
entrecôte	ribsteak
faux filet	sirloin steak
lapin	rabbit
mouton	mutton
poulet	chicken
veau	veal

Légumes	Vegetables
ail	garlic
champignons	mushrooms
chou	cabbage
concombre	cucumber
laitue	lettuce
maïs	corn
oignon	onion
petits pois	peas
pois chiches	chickpeas
poivron	sweet pepper or capsicum
pomme de terre	potato
riz	rice

Fruits & Noix	Fruit & Nuts
amandes	almonds
cacahouètes	peanuts
cerises	cherries
fraises	strawberries
noisettes	hazelnuts
noix	walnuts
orange	orange
pamplemousse	grapefruit
pastèque	watermelon
pêche	peach
poire	pear
pomme	apple
raisins	grapes

Boissons	Drinks
un café	a short black coffee
un grand/petit crème	a large/small milk coffee
un jus de pamplemousee	a grapefruit juice
un jus d'orange	an orange juice
un thé	a cup of tea
thé au citron/au lait	lemon/white tea

Vins	Wines
blanc	white
brut	very dry
demi-sec	sweet
doux	very sweet
méthode champenoise	mature and sparkling
mousseux	sparkling
rouge	red
sec	dry
vin de table/vin ordinaire	table wine

Essential Groceries

bread	**dü pã**	*du pain*
butter	**dü berr**	*du beurre*
cereal	**der la se-re-al**	*de la céréale*
cheese	**dü froh-mazh**	*du fromage*
chocolate	**dü shok-o-la**	*du chocolat*
coffee	**dü ka-fe**	*du café*
matches	**deiz a-lü-met**	*des allumettes*
milk	**dü leh**	*du lai*
mineral water	**der loh mee-ne-ral**	*de l'eau minérale*
fruit	**dei frwee**	*des fruits*
soap	**dü sa-võ**	*du savon*
sugar	**dü sükr**	*du sucre*
tea	**dü te**	*du thé*
toilet paper	**dü pa-pye ee-zhye-neek**	*du papier hygiénique*
toothpaste	**dü dã-tee-frees**	*du dentifrice*
washing powder	**la les-eev**	*la lessive*
yoghurt	**ya-oot**	*yaourt*

Numbers & Amounts

1	**en**	*un*
2	**der**	*deux*
3	**twa**	*trois*
4	**katr**	*quatre*
5	**senk**	*cinq*
6	**sees**	*six*
7	**seht**	*sept*
8	**weet**	*huit*
9	**nerf**	*neuf*
10	**dees**	*dix*

More World Food Titles

Brimming with cultural insight, the World Food series takes the guesswork out of new cuisines and provide the ideal guides to your own culinary adventures. The books cover everything to do with food and drink in each country – the history and evolution of the cuisine, its staples & specialities, and the kitchen philosophy of the people. You'll find definitive two-way dictionaries, menu readers and useful phrases for shopping, drunken apologies and much more.

The essential guides for travelling and non-travelling food lovers around the world, look out for the full range of World Food titles including:

Italy,
Mexico,
Spain,
Thailand,
Turkey,
Vietnam,
Deep South (USA),
France,
Ireland &
Hong Kong.

Out to Eat Series

Lonely Planet's Out to Eat series takes its food seriously but offers a fresh approach with independent, unstuffy opinion on hundreds of hand-picked restaurants, bars and cafes in each city. Along with reviews, Out to Eat identifies the best culinary cul-de-sacs, describes cultural contexts of ethnic cuisines, and explains menu terms and ingredients.

Updated annually, new Out to Eat titles include:
Melbourne, Paris, Sydney, London and San Francisco.

Planet Talk

Our FREE quarterly printed newsletter is full of tips from travellers and anecdotes from Lonely Planet guidebook authors. Every issue is packed with up-to-date travel news and advice, and includes:

- a postcard from Lonely Planet co-founder Tony Wheeler
- a swag of mail from travellers
- a look at life on the road through the eyes of a Lonely Planet author
- topical health advice
- prizes for the best travel yarn
- news about forthcoming Lonely Planet events
- a complete list of Lonely Planet books and other titles

To join our mailing list, residents of the UK, Europe and Africa can email us at go@lonelyplanet.co.uk; residents of North and South America can do so at info@lonelyplanet.com; the rest of the world can email talk2us@lonelyplanet.com.au, or contact any Lonely Planet office.

The Lonely Planet Story

Lonely Planet published its first book in 1973 in response to the numerous 'How did you do it?' questions Maureen and Tony Wheeler were asked after driving, bussing, hitching, sailing and railing their way from England to Australia. Written at a kitchen table and hand collated, trimmed and stapled, *Across Asia on the Cheap* became an instant local bestseller.

Eighteen months in South-East Asia resulted in their second guide, *South-East Asia on a Shoestring*, which they put together in a backstreet Chinese hotel in Singapore in 1975. The 'yellow bible', as it quickly became known to backpackers around the world, soon became the guide to the region. It has sold well over ¾ million copies and is now in its 10th edition, still retaining its familiar yellow cover.

Today there are over 400 titles, including travel guides, walking guides, language kits & phrasebooks, travel atlases & maps, diving guides, restaurant guides, first time travel guides, condensed guides, illustrated pictorials and travel literature. The company is the largest independent travel publisher in the world.

The emphasis continues to be on travel for independent travellers. Tony and Maureen still travel for several months of each year and play an active part in the writing, updating and quality control of Lonely Planet's guides.

They have been joined by over 120 authors and over 400 staff at our offices in Melbourne (Australia), Oakland (USA), London (UK) and Paris (France). Travellers themselves also make a valuable contribution to the guides through the feedback we receive in thousands of letters each year and on our web site.

The people at Lonely Planet strongly believe that travellers can make a positive contribution to the countries they visit, both through their appreciation of the countries' culture, wildlife and natural features, and through the money they spend. In addition, the company makes a direct contribution to the countries and regions it covers. Since 1986 a percentage of the income from each book has been donated to ventures such as famine relief in Africa; aid projects in India; agricultural projects in Central America; Greenpeace's efforts to halt French nuclear testing in the Pacific.

Lonely Planet Offices

Australia
PO Box 617, Hawthorn, Victoria 3122
☎ 03-9819 1877
fax 03-9819 6459
email:talk2us@lonelyplanet.com.au

USA
150 Linden St, Oakland, CA 94607
☎ 510-893 8555 TOLL FREE: 800 275 8555
fax 510-893 8572
email: info@lonelyplanet.com

UK
10a Spring Place, London NW5 3BH
☎ 020-7428 4800
fax 020-7428 4828
email: go@lonelyplanet.co.uk

France
1 rue du Dahomey, 75011 Paris
☎ 01 55 25 33 00
fax 01 55 25 33 01
email: bip@lonelyplanet.fr